CGP's formula for success in Reasoning!

The KS2 SATs Reasoning papers can be a tricky operation... but don't worry — this practice-packed CGP book will get all your skills in order.

There are realistic questions for every Reasoning topic, plus all the answers are included. And what's more, there's a progress chart for marking your work and spotting where you need more practice. Handy!

We've even included a practice test at the end of the book, perfect for making sure you're ready for the real thing!

What CGP is all about

Our sole aim here at CGP is to produce the highest quality books — carefully written, immaculately presented and dangerously close to being funny.

Then we work our socks off to get them out to you — at the cheapest possible prices.

Contents

Section One — Number & Place Value

Place Value and Ordering Numbers 2
Negative Numbers 3
Roman Numerals 4
Decimals 5
Rounding 6
Mixed Practice 7

Section Two — Calculations

Adding and Subtracting 8
Multiplying and Dividing 10
Order of Operations 12
Checking and Estimating 13
Multiples, Factors and Primes 14
Mixed Practice 15

Section Three — Fractions, Decimals & Percentages

Fractions 16
Comparing Fractions 17
Adding and Subtracting Fractions 18
Multiplying and Dividing Fractions 19
Fractions, Decimals and Percentages 20
Mixed Practice 21

Section Four — Ratio, Proportion & Algebra

Ratio, Proportion and Unequal Sharing 22
Percentage Problems 24
Formulas and Combinations 25
Finding Missing Numbers 26
Number Sequences 27
Mixed Practice 28

Section Five — Measurement

Units and Conversion 29
Time 30
Money 31
Perimeter and Area 32
Volume 34
Mixed Practice 35

Section Six — Geometry

Angle Rules 36
2D Shapes 37
Angles in Shapes 38
3D Shapes 39
Coordinates 40
Reflection and Translation 41
Mixed Practice 42

Section Seven — Statistics

Tables and Pictograms 43
Bar Charts and Line Graphs 44
Pie Charts 46
The Mean 47
Mixed Practice 48

Practice Test 49
Answers 55
Progress Chart 62

Published by CGP

Editors: Martha Bozic, Samuel Mann, Tom Miles

With thanks to Simon Little and Clare Selway
for the proofreading.
Also thanks to Jan Greenway for the copyright research.

*Contains public sector information licensed under the
Open Government Licence v3.0.
http://www.nationalarchives.gov.uk/doc/open-government-licence/version/3/*

ISBN: 978 1 78908 613 3

Printed by W&G Baird Ltd, Antrim.
Clipart from Corel®

Based on the classic CGP style created by Richard Parsons.

Text, design, layout and original illustrations
© Coordination Group Publications Ltd. (CGP) 2020
All rights reserved.

**Photocopying this book is not permitted, even if you have a CLA licence.
Extra copies are available from CGP with next day delivery • 0800 1712 712 • www.cgpbooks.co.uk**

Section One — Number & Place Value

Place Value and Ordering Numbers

1) Look at the number 6 831 527.

What digit is in the hundred thousands place?

1 mark

What is the value of the 5?

1 mark

2) Write the smallest number below in words.

249   294   427   247

1 mark

3) Put these numbers in **ascending** order.

5378   5353   5296   5359

1 mark

4) Write in the missing digits to make this addition correct.

5 ☐ 4 + 6 ☐ = 654

1 mark

5) Write **in digits** the number that is one thousand more than one hundred and ninety nine thousand.

1 mark

"I can read, write, order and compare numbers up to ten million, and work out the value of each digit."

Negative Numbers

1 Fill in the missing numbers on the number line below.

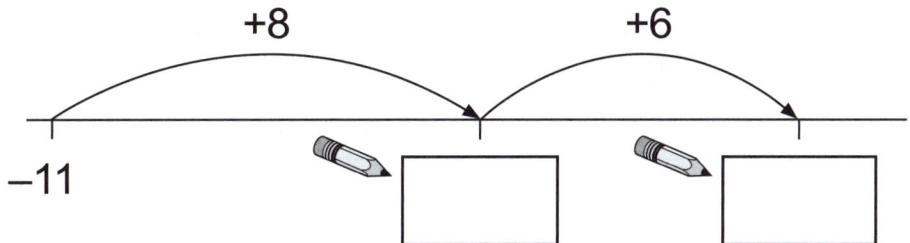

2 marks

2 Dinah stands on a diving board 5 m above water level.
She dives down to 3 m below water level.

How many metres does she dive down from the diving board?

 m

1 mark

3 The temperature in Jay's garden is –4 °C at midnight and 11 °C **warmer** at midday.

What is the temperature in Jay's garden at midday?

 °C

1 mark

4 Kobe parks on floor –9 of an underground car park.
He has to go up 5 floors to get to the ticket machine.

On what number floor is the ticket machine?

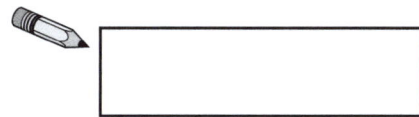

1 mark

5 Write **<**, **>** or **=** in the box to make this number sentence correct.

–13 + 8 ☐ 2 – 7

1 mark

"I can calculate using negative numbers."

Section One — Number & Place Value

Roman Numerals

1 Claudius records the number of cups of tea he makes over three days in the table below.

Monday	Tuesday	Wednesday
XVI	VII	IX

Write the number of cups of tea he made on Monday in digits.

1 mark

How many more cups of tea did he make on Wednesday than on Tuesday?

1 mark

2 Find the missing Roman numeral below.

C?I = 151

? =

1 mark

3 Tim finds a scroll from the year MCCLXI.

Write this year as a number.

1 mark

4 Malik will turn 90 years old in the year MMXCII.

In which year was Malik **born**? Circle your answer.

1992   2002   2011   2012   2092

1 mark

"I can read Roman numerals up to M and recognise years written in Roman numerals."

Decimals

1 Look at the number 0.759.

Which digit is in the hundredths place?

1 mark

2 Circle the smallest amount of money below.

£1.95   £1.99   £1.98   £1.89

1 mark

3 Write < or > in the boxes to complete the number sentences.

0.008 ☐ 0.03

0.96 ☐ 0.908

1.387 ☐ 1.41

3 marks

4 Ellen's ladder is 4.59 m tall and Clark's ladder is 4.7 m tall.

Whose ladder is taller?

1 mark

5 Put these decimals in order from smallest to largest.

0.34   0.339   0.332   0.43

2 marks

"I can identify the value of each digit to three decimal places. I can order and compare numbers with up to three decimal places."

Section One — Number & Place Value

Rounding

1 Round the number 927 413:

to the nearest ten   to the nearest ten thousand

[   ]   [   ]

1 mark

2 Round each of these numbers to the nearest hundred:

748 → [   ]   4091 → [   ]

1 mark

3 What is 6 319 657 rounded to the nearest thousand?

Circle the correct answer.

6 319 700   6 320 000   6 319 000   6 310 000

1 mark

4 Jona's house is 8.39 m tall.

Round this height to the nearest metre.

[   ] m

1 mark

5 Which two of these decimals round to the same number when they are rounded to one decimal place?

2.48   2.41   2.52   2.55

[   ] and [   ]

1 mark

"I can round any whole number. I can round decimal numbers to one decimal place or the nearest whole number."

Section One — Number & Place Value   © CGP — Not to be photocopied

Mixed Practice

That's the end of Number & Place Value — test how much you've learnt with these questions.

1 There are two hundred and thirty-eight thousand, eight hundred and fifty-five miles between the moon and the Earth.

Write this distance in digits.

1 mark

2 Ally's sunflower is 2.25 m tall.

How tall is her sunflower to one decimal place?

m

1 mark

3 Which is bigger: MCMXXV or 2021?

1 mark

4 Ciaran and Kerry are playing a game. In each round the winner gains 3 points and the loser gets 5 points taken away.

They play 5 rounds and Kerry wins 2 of them.
How many points does she have in total?

2 marks

Check how well you've done with Number & Place Value by adding up your marks from this Mixed Practice page. Write your score in the box on the right, then fill in the scoresheet at the end of the book.

/ 5

Section Two — Calculations

Adding and Subtracting

1 Fill in the missing digits to make the calculation correct.

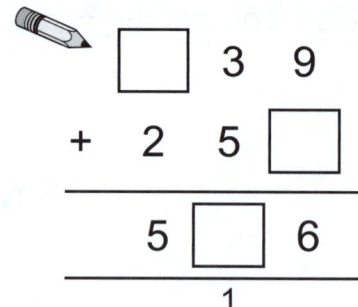

```
    ☐ 3 9
+   2 5 ☐
  ─────────
    5 ☐ 6
      1
```

1 mark

2 There are 9415 tickets available for a rock concert.
761 tickets are sold in the hour after they go on sale.

How many tickets are left?

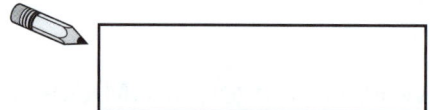

1 mark

3 Write in the missing digits to make this calculation correct.

8 ☐ 3 − 9 ☐ = 742

1 mark

4 Paula grows 7985 kg of potatoes on her farm.
She sells 4030 kg to the greengrocers and 2108 kg at the market.

How many kilograms of potatoes does she have left?

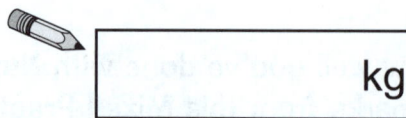 kg

2 marks

Adding and Subtracting

5 Fill in the missing digits to make the subtraction correct.

```
   2 8 . 6 ☐
 - 1 0 . ☐ 8
   ─────────
   1 ☐ . 8 2
```

1 mark

6 Mollie buys one of each item shown below.

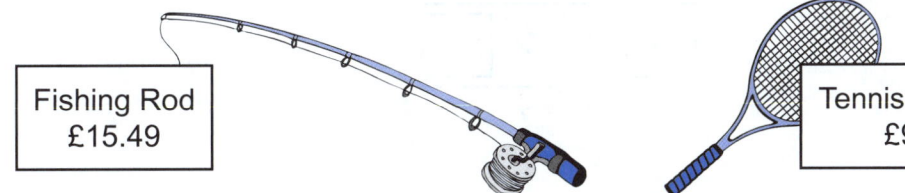

Fishing Rod £15.49   Tennis Racquet £9.99

Using a mental method, work out how much Mollie pays in total.

£ ☐

1 mark

She pays with £40. Using a mental method, work out how much change she gets.

£ ☐

1 mark

7 Manuel swims three lengths of a pool in exactly one minute. His first length takes 19.76 s and his second length is 22.14 s.

How long did he take to swim the third length?

☐ s

2 marks

"I can add and subtract large numbers mentally and using standard written methods."

Multiplying and Dividing

1) Circle the correct answer to 513 ÷ 1000.

5.13   0.513   0.5013   0.0513

1 mark

2) Fill in the missing digits to complete the multiplication.

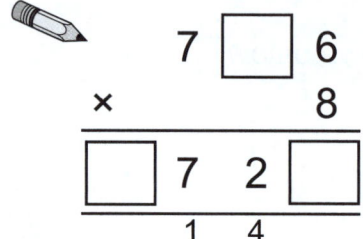

1 mark

3) Fill in the missing numbers in the function machines below.

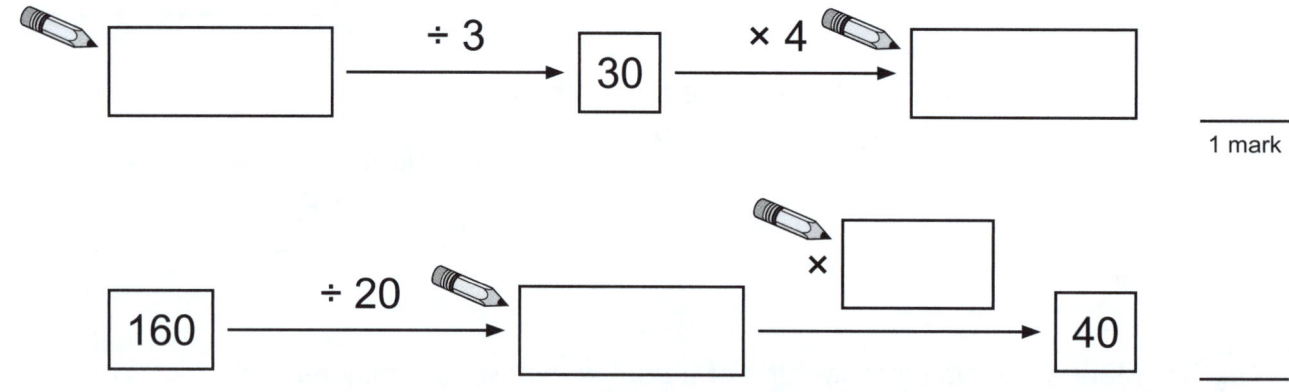

1 mark

1 mark

4) Jasmine buys theme park tickets for herself and two friends.

She pays £18.99. How much does one ticket cost?

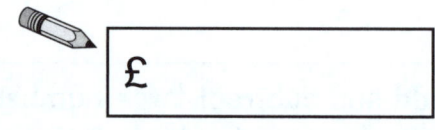

£

1 mark

Section Two — Calculations

Multiplying and Dividing

5 Jackie has 840 beads. She needs 9 beads to make one bracelet.

How many bracelets can she make?

1 mark

How many beads will she have left over?

1 mark

6 Mas orders 27 boxes of bananas to sell in his shop.
There are 5 bananas in a bunch and 15 bunches in a box.

How many bananas does he order in total?

2 marks

7 Gino is filling bottles with ink. He has 2666 ml of ink.

Each bottle can hold 14 ml of ink.
How many bottles can he completely fill?

2 marks

"I can multiply and divide numbers mentally and using standard written methods. I can multiply and divide decimals by whole numbers."

Order of Operations

1) A pair of brackets is missing from the calculation below. Write the calculation with the brackets to make it correct.

3 × 7 − 2 + 8 = 23

1 mark

2) Keira thinks that 6 + 3 × 5 − 9 = 36.

Show that she is **not** correct.

1 mark

3) Draw lines to match up each calculation with the correct answer.

| $12 - 2^2 \div 2$ | $(12 - 2^2) \div 2$ | $12 \div 2^2 - 2$ |

| 4 | 10 | 1 |

2 marks

4) The menu at a bakery is shown on the right. Jesse buys a cream bun for himself and one eclair for each of his 3 friends.

How much change does he get from £10?

Cream bun 70p
Cupcake £1.10
Eclair £1.20

£ _____

2 marks

"I can work out what calculations I need to use to solve a problem. I know the order to do things in a calculation."

Section Two — Calculations

Checking and Estimating

1 By estimating, circle the correct answer to 60.27 ÷ 4.9.

10.13   12.3   14.23   15.3

1 mark

2 Sakura calculates 752 ÷ 47 = 16.

Write down a calculation she could do to check her answer.

☐ × ☐ = ☐

1 mark

3 Obi thinks that 983 × 79 = 784 657.

Use estimation to decide whether his answer looks correct.

1 mark

4 Ms Wills needs to buy workbooks for each pupil in 11 classes of 33 pupils. She works out that she needs to buy 11 × 33 = 363 workbooks.

Use an inverse operation to show that she is correct.

1 mark

"I can estimate to check the answer to a calculation.
I can use inverse operations to check answers."

Multiples, Factors and Primes

1) Look at the numbers below.

1   2   4   7   9   11   14

Which of these numbers are factors of 28?

[   ]

1 mark

Which of these numbers are prime?

[   ]

1 mark

2) What are the common factors of 12 and 30?

[   ]

2 marks

3) What number between 40 and 50 is a multiple of 7 and has a factor of 6?

[   ]

1 mark

4) Find the common multiple of 6 and 9 that is less than 20.

[   ]

1 mark

5) Find three prime numbers which multiply together to make 165.

[   ] [   ] [   ]

2 marks

"I know how to find common multiples, common factors, prime numbers and prime factors."

Section Two — Calculations

Mixed Practice

That's the end of Calculations — test how much you've learnt with these questions.

1) Layton is thinking of a prime number that is a factor of 22, 44 and 66.

What two numbers could his number be?

☐ and ☐

1 mark

2) 81 × 989 = 80 109. What is 8.1 × 9.89?

☐

1 mark

3) A sun hat costs £4.59 and an ice cream costs £2.70. Fatima wants to buy a sun hat and three ice creams.

She has a £10 note. How much more money does she need?

£ ☐

2 marks

4) A factory produces 9360 biscuits in one day.

There are 22 biscuits in a pack. How many biscuits are left over after every pack has been filled?

☐

2 marks

Check how well you've done with Calculations by adding up your marks from this Mixed Practice page. Write your score in the box on the right, then fill in the scoresheet at the end of the book.

/ 6

Section Three — Fractions, Decimals & Percentages

Fractions

1) Fill in the missing numbers to make these sets of fractions equivalent.

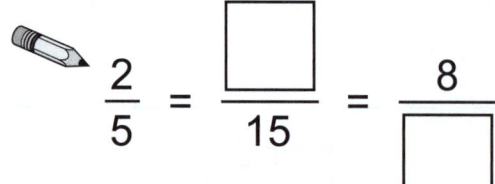   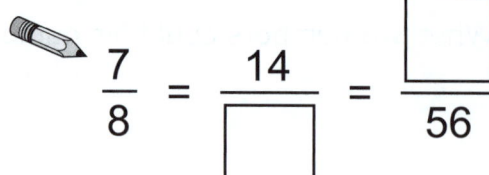

2 marks

2) Circle all of the fractions below that are equivalent to $\frac{4}{7}$.

$\frac{12}{28}$ $\frac{28}{35}$ $\frac{8}{14}$ $\frac{7}{4}$ $\frac{12}{21}$

1 mark

3) The shapes below are split into equal parts. A fraction of the hexagon has been shaded.

Shade the rectangle and triangle so that each has the same fraction shaded as the hexagon.

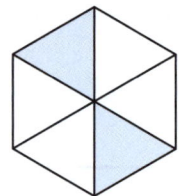   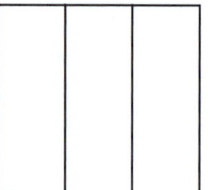   

1 mark

4) Draw lines to match each improper fraction to the equivalent mixed number.

One has been done for you.

$\frac{23}{4}$ $\frac{18}{4}$ $\frac{13}{4}$ $\frac{41}{4}$ $\frac{11}{4}$

$10\frac{1}{4}$ $2\frac{3}{4}$ $5\frac{3}{4}$ $4\frac{1}{2}$ $3\frac{1}{4}$

2 marks

"I can swap between mixed numbers and improper fractions. I can simplify fractions and find equivalent fractions."

Comparing Fractions

1 Put the fractions below in order from smallest to largest.

$\frac{2}{3}$ $\frac{3}{4}$ $\frac{7}{12}$

☐ ☐ ☐
smallest   largest

1 mark

2 Circle the smaller fraction in each pair below.

$\frac{4}{9}$ or $\frac{7}{18}$ $\frac{45}{77}$ or $\frac{6}{11}$ $\frac{7}{8}$ or $\frac{60}{72}$

2 marks

3 Write **<**, **>** or **=** in each box to make these number sentences correct.

$\frac{7}{8}$ ☐ $\frac{19}{24}$ $\frac{14}{49}$ ☐ $\frac{3}{7}$

2 marks

4 Circle all of the fractions below that are **larger** than $\frac{5}{6}$.

$\frac{8}{24}$ $\frac{2}{3}$ $\frac{4}{5}$ $\frac{11}{6}$ $\frac{9}{10}$

2 marks

5 Write each of these fractions in the correct box to make the number sentence correct.

$\frac{18}{45}$ $\frac{7}{5}$ $\frac{24}{30}$

☐ > ☐ > ☐

1 mark

"I can compare and order fractions, including fractions greater than 1."

Adding and Subtracting Fractions

1 Joanne ate $\frac{1}{4}$ of a pie and her parents ate $\frac{6}{10}$, as shown on the diagram.

What fraction of the pie have they eaten altogether?

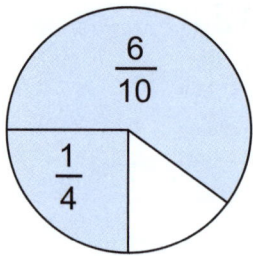

1 mark

2 Nisan has read $\frac{4}{7}$ of a book. Paris has read $\frac{2}{3}$ of the same book.

How much more of the book has Paris read?

1 mark

3 In a box of chocolates, $\frac{1}{5}$ are milk chocolate and $\frac{3}{8}$ are dark chocolate.

What fraction of the chocolates in the box are neither milk nor dark chocolate?

2 marks

4 Klaus walks $1\frac{3}{4}$ miles to the bus station.
He gets on a bus and stays on it for $5\frac{1}{6}$ miles.

How many miles does he travel in total?
Give your answer as a mixed number.

miles

2 marks

"I can add and subtract fractions by finding a common denominator."

Multiplying and Dividing Fractions

1 What is $\frac{2}{7}$ of 280 g?

g

1 mark

2 3 identical cucumbers weigh $\frac{5}{8}$ kg. How much does 1 cucumber weigh?

kg

1 mark

3 Fill in the missing fractions in the function machines below.

☐ —÷ 2→ $\frac{2}{9}$ —× 5→ ☐

2 marks

☐ —× 6→ $\frac{4}{5}$ —× $\frac{3}{7}$→ ☐

2 marks

4 Dan fills 24 fish tanks each with $25\frac{3}{4}$ litres of water.

What is the total volume of the water in the tanks?

litres

2 marks

"I can multiply fractions by whole numbers and by other fractions. I can divide fractions by whole numbers."

Fractions, Decimals and Percentages

1 Which of the values below is equivalent to 0.03? Circle the correct answer.

$\frac{3}{10}$ $\frac{100}{3}$ 30% $\frac{1}{3}$ $\frac{3}{100}$

1 mark

2 Write **<**, **>** or **=** in each box to make these number sentences correct.

15% ☐ 0.4 $\frac{17}{10}$ ☐ 1.07

1 mark

3 Hope has completed 12 out of 25 levels in a video game.

What percentage of the levels has she completed?

☐ %

1 mark

4 Beth gets 36 out of 50 questions correct in a quiz.
Jordan gets 75% of the questions correct.

Who got the most questions correct? Show your working.

2 marks

5 Arlo drinks $\frac{107}{200}$ of a litre of squash.

Write this fraction as a decimal.

1 mark

"I can convert between fractions, decimals and percentages."

Mixed Practice

That's the end of Fractions, Decimals & Percentages — test how much you've learnt with these questions.

1 The rule for this sequence is add $\frac{2}{3}$ each time. Fill in the missing terms.

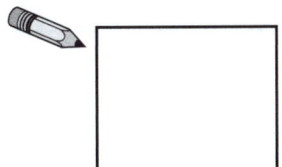 $3\frac{1}{3}$ 4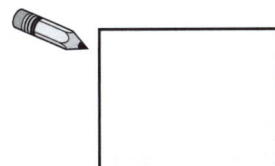

2 marks

2 A group of friends have $\frac{4}{9}$ of a cake left. What fraction of the full cake does each person get if the remaining cake is shared between:

5 people?    8 people?

2 marks

3 Write each of these fractions as an equivalent fraction.

Your answers should have the **same denominator**.

$\frac{3}{8} =$  $\frac{6}{7} =$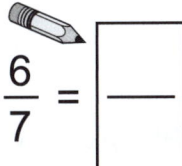

2 marks

4 Put these values in order from largest to smallest.

$\frac{60}{100}$ 8% $\frac{1}{10}$ 0.65 $\frac{4}{5}$

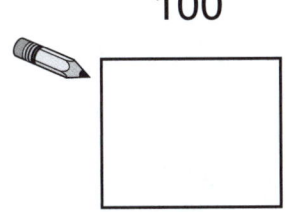 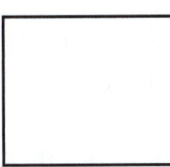 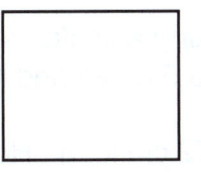 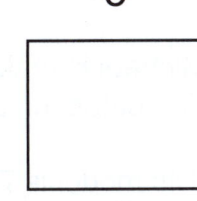

largest ⟶ smallest   2 marks

Check how well you've done with Fractions, Decimals & Percentages by adding up your marks from this Mixed Practice page. Write your score in the box on the right, then fill in the scoresheet at the end of the book.   / 8

Section Four — Ratio, Proportion & Algebra

Ratio, Proportion and Unequal Sharing

1) 2 melons cost £3 at the supermarket. How much would 8 melons cost?

£ ☐

1 mark

2) Kirkdale and Grisby are 10 miles apart in real life.
They are drawn on a map where 3 cm represents 2 miles.

How far apart are they drawn on the map?

☐ cm

1 mark

3) The ratio of blue to yellow flowers in Raja's garden is 1:6.

There are 3 blue flowers in her garden.
How many yellow flowers are there?

☐

1 mark

4) Two plates weigh the same as five bowls.

One bowl weighs 200 g. How much does one plate weigh?

☐ g

1 mark

5) Michael is making a scale model of a dinosaur.
The dinosaur is 5 m tall and 12 m long.

His model is 72 cm long. How tall is his model?

☐ cm

1 mark

Ratio, Proportion and Unequal Sharing

6 Hilda lines up 6 identical toy cars in a row as shown below.

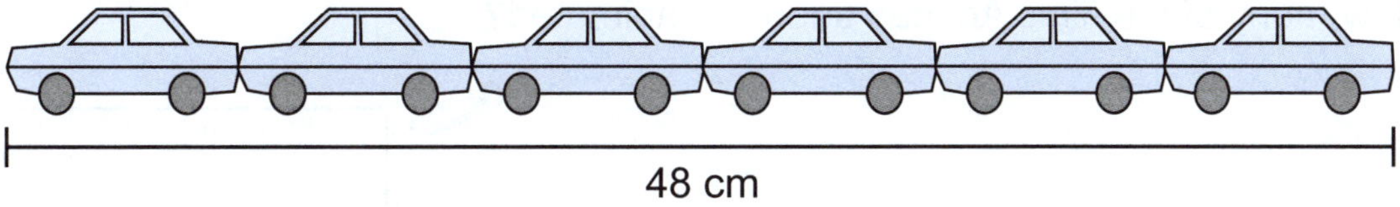

48 cm

She adds on 5 more cars to the row.
How long is the row of cars now?

[ ] cm

2 marks

7 Liam fills 8 identical watering cans with a total of 72 litres of water.

How many litres of water do 3 watering cans contain?

[ ] litres

1 mark

8 Look at the two lines drawn below.

Line X: 4 cm

Line Y: 12 cm

What is the ratio of the length
of line X to the length of line Y?

[:]

1 mark

9 Vic and Pearl share £30. For every £2 Vic gets, Pearl gets £3.

How much money does each of them get?

Vic: £ [ ]   Pearl: £ [ ]

2 marks

"I can solve problems to do with the relative sizes of two amounts. I can work out how to share things unequally. I can use scaling to solve money and shape problems."

Percentage Problems

1 Adi has seen 120 films. 40% of them are animated.

How many of the films Adi has seen are animated?

1 mark

2 A lorry is carrying 320 chocolate eggs. 55% of the eggs melt on the journey.

How many of the chocolate eggs did **not** melt?

1 mark

3 Nicola recorded the colours of the cars at a car park in the table below. Complete the table to show what **percentage** of the cars were each colour.

Colour	Number	Percentage of total
Blue	8	%
Red	15	%
Silver	2	%

2 marks

4 Bob has 41 yellow marbles and 9 green marbles.
Katya has 16 yellow marbles and 4 green marbles.

Who has the lower **percentage** of green marbles?

2 marks

"I can find a percentage of an amount.
I can use percentages to compare amounts."

Formulas and Combinations

1 Gary scored 4 goals in a game of football.
Fiona scored *n* times as many goals as Gary.

Circle the expression that shows the number of goals that Fiona scored.

$4 \div n$ $4 + n$ $4 - n$ $4 \times n$ $n \div 4$

1 mark

2 As part of a deal, customers at a cafe can choose to have any two of these items: apple, crisps, sandwich and soup.

There are 6 possible combinations. Which two are missing from this list?

| Apple and crisps | Apple and soup |
| Crisps and sandwich | Sandwich and soup |

[ ] and [ ]

[ ] and [ ]

1 mark

3 A pizza takeaway uses this formula to work out how much to charge its customers: Price = number of pizzas × £6 + £3.50

Sifa orders 3 pizzas.
How much will she be charged?

£ [ ]

1 mark

Ant is charged £45.50.
How many pizzas did he order?

[ ]

2 marks

"I can use formulas written in words. I can list all possible combinations of different options."

Finding Missing Numbers

1 Leanne multiplies her age by 8 and adds 5 to get 101.

How many years old is Leanne?

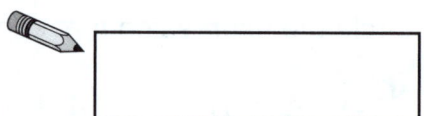

1 mark

2 ☐ = 45 − △

What is the value of ☐ when △ = 27?

☐ =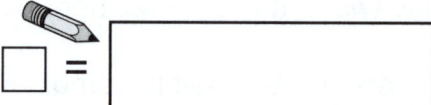

1 mark

What is the value of △ when ☐ = 11?

△ =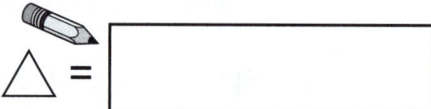

1 mark

3 64 ÷ X = Y

X and Y are positive whole numbers greater than 1. X isn't equal to Y.
Give a possible pair of values for X and Y.

X =    Y =

1 mark

4 Look at the patterns below. Each shape in the pattern has a value.

Work out the value of each shape.

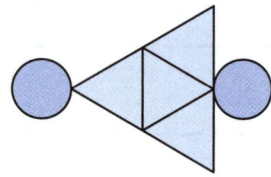 Pattern A = 186   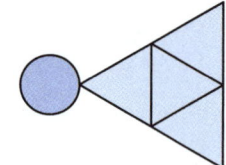 Pattern B = 141

○ =    △ =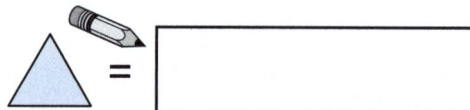

2 marks

"I can solve missing number problems using symbols and letters. I can find pairs of numbers to solve problems with two unknowns."

Section Four — Ratio, Proportion & Algebra   © CGP — Not to be photocopied

Number Sequences

1 The numbers in this sequence increase by the same amount each time.

Write down the next two terms of this sequence.

9   16   23   [ ]   [ ]

1 mark

2 The numbers in this sequence decrease by the same amount each time.

Fill in the missing terms in the sequence.

89 357   [ ]   89 157   89 057   [ ]

1 mark

3 The numbers in this sequence increase by 23 each time.

Fill in the missing terms.

[ ]   50   [ ]   96   [ ]

2 marks

4 Use this rule to fill in the missing terms in the sequence:
"Divide by the same number each time."

[ ]   250   50   [ ]   [ ]

2 marks

5 The rule for this sequence is "multiply by 2, then subtract 5".

Fill in the missing terms.

30   55   [ ]   [ ]

2 marks

"I can make and describe number sequences."

Mixed Practice

That's the end of Ratio, Proportion & Algebra — test how much you've learnt with these questions.

1 Noah is scaling up a recipe for biscuits. Work out the missing amounts.

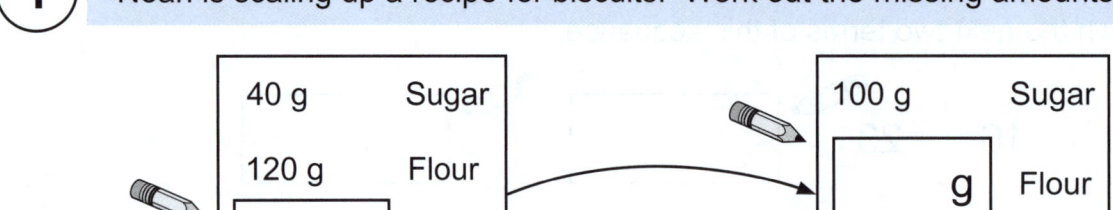

2 marks

2 The numbers in this sequence decrease by the same number each time.

Fill in the missing terms.

81   64

2 marks

3 13% of 2100 teachers don't drink tea. How many teachers is this?

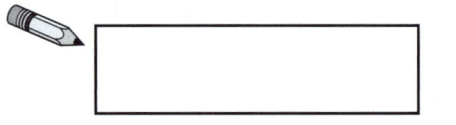

1 mark

4 A shop uses this formula to work out how much to charge for birdseed:

Cost = 50p × weight of birdseed in kg + 30p

Nessa spends £5.30 on birdseed.
How many kg of birdseed did she buy?

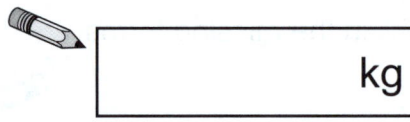 kg

2 marks

Check how well you've done with Ratio, Proportion & Algebra by adding up your marks from this Mixed Practice page. Write your score in the box on the right, then fill in the scoresheet at the end of the book.   / 7

Section Five — Measurement

Units and Conversion

1) Circle the length that is equivalent to 42 cm.

4.2 m   4200 mm   0.42 m   4.2 mm

1 mark

2) Jess has 1.2 kg of flour. She needs 400 g to make one loaf.

How many loaves of bread can she make?

1 mark

3) The heights of Adeola's brothers are shown below.

Put their heights in order from shortest to tallest.

131 cm   0.98 m   1.4 m   119 cm

1 mark

Adeola is exactly 5 feet tall. 1 foot ≈ 30 cm.
Work out her approximate height in metres.

_____ m

1 mark

4) Monroe pours 750 ml out of a 4.5 litre tank of water.

What volume of water is left in the tank, in ml?

_____ ml

1 mark

5) Kayleigh lives 15 miles away from her grandmother. 5 miles ≈ 8 km.

Approximately how many **kilometres** away does Kayleigh live from her grandmother?

_____ km

1 mark

"I can convert between units of length, mass and volume, and between miles and kilometres."

Time

1 Draw lines to match up each pair of equivalent times.

2 hours	6 days
10 minutes	60 hours
2.5 days	120 minutes
144 hours	600 seconds

2 marks

2 Otis went on holiday on the 22nd July and returned on 12th August.

How many weeks was Otis on holiday for?

 weeks

1 mark

3 Darren starts school at 8:30 am and finishes at 3:15 pm.

How many minutes does Darren spend at school each day?

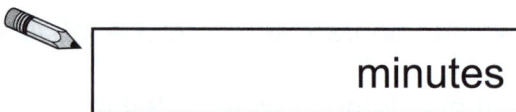 minutes

2 marks

4 Sarah starts driving one morning at the time shown on the clock. She drives for 2 hours and 47 minutes.

What time does she stop driving?
Give your answer in 24-hour clock format.

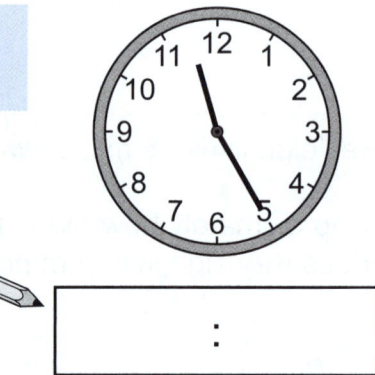

2 marks

"I can convert between units of time.
I can solve problems involving time."

Section Five — Measurement

Money

1 Jan collects 5037 pence for charity.

How much does she collect in pounds?

£ _____

1 mark

2 Deo has £5 to spend on holiday. He buys a postcard for 90p and a stamp for £1.22.

How much money does he have left?

£ _____

1 mark

3 Gaina puts 80p into her piggy bank each week.

How much money will she put in her piggy bank in 8 weeks?

£ _____

1 mark

4 Krishnan buys 4 posters for £4.80.

How much would 7 posters cost?

£ _____

1 mark

5 Isla buys a jumper at half price. She pays with a £10 note and gets £3.25 change.

What was the **original** price of the jumper?

£ _____

2 marks

"I can solve problems involving money."

Perimeter and Area

1) A square has a side length of 12 cm. What is the area of the square?

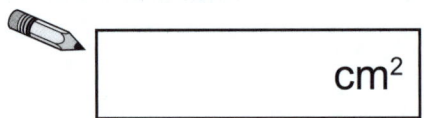 cm²

1 mark

2) Look at the shapes on the grid below. Each square on the grid is 1 cm².

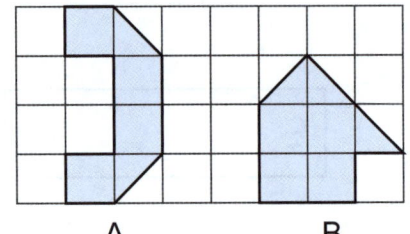

A   B

Work out which shape has the greater area. Write this area in the answer box below.

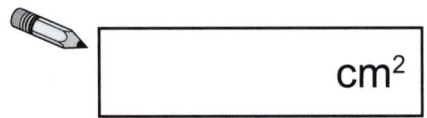 cm²

1 mark

3) Joey makes a hexagon out of six equilateral triangles.

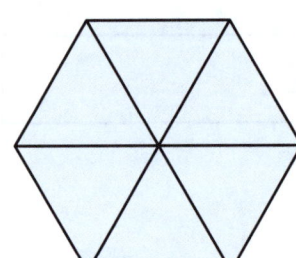

The perimeter of one triangle is 21 cm. What is the perimeter of the hexagon?

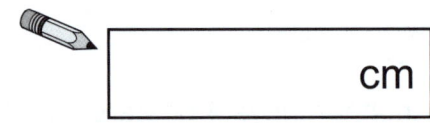 cm

1 mark

4) The floor plan for Amy's apartment is shown below.

What is the area of Amy's lounge?

 m²

1 mark

Amy wants to put a single row of 10 cm wide tiles all the way around the kitchen walls. How many tiles will she need?

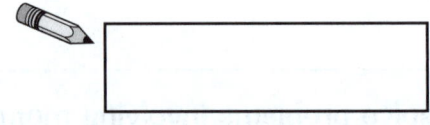

2 marks

Section Five — Measurement

Perimeter and Area

5 Draw a rectangle which has an area of 36 cm² and a perimeter of 30 cm on the grid below.

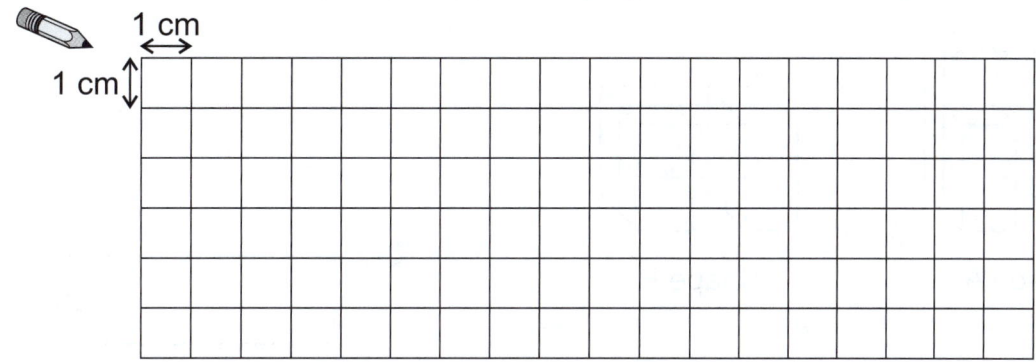

2 marks

6 Alok arranges two identical parallelogram tiles to make an arrow.

The height of each parallelogram is 2.5 cm.
What is the area of Alok's arrow?

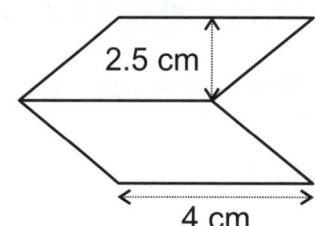

 cm²

2 marks

7 The triangle and rectangle below have the same area.

Work out the perimeter of the rectangle. The shapes are not to scale.

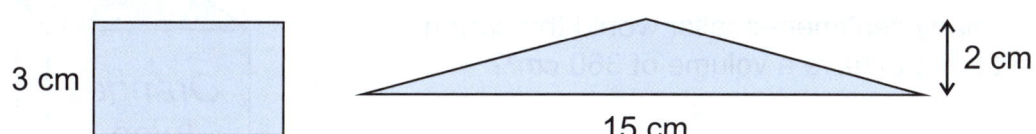

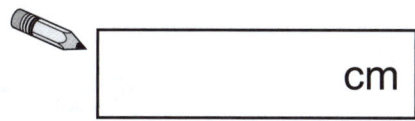 cm

2 marks

"I can measure and calculate the perimeters and areas of shapes. I know that shapes with the same area can have different perimeters and vice versa."

Volume

1 Jake builds these shapes using 1 cm³ cubes.

What is the difference in volume between the two shapes?

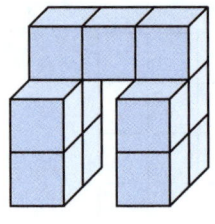
Shape A

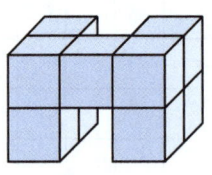
Shape B

☐ cm³

1 mark

2 Dionne makes a cuboid from this net.

What is the volume of Dionne's cuboid?

☐ cm³

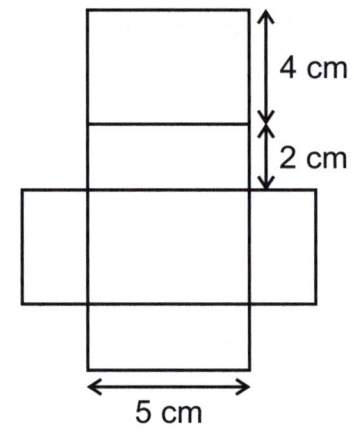
4 cm
2 cm
5 cm

1 mark

3 A juice carton has the dimensions shown on the right.

How many centimetres taller would the carton need to be to have a volume of 360 cm³?

☐ cm

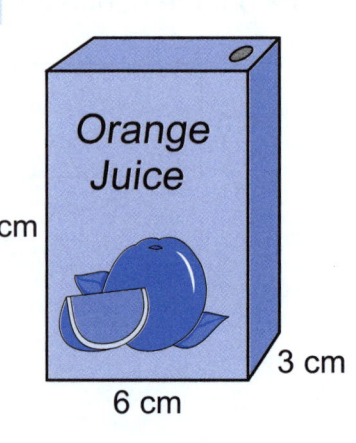
Orange Juice
10 cm
6 cm
3 cm

2 marks

"I can calculate the volumes of cubes and cuboids."

Section Five — Measurement

Mixed Practice

That's the end of Measurement — test how much you've learnt with these questions.

1) Circle the cuboid below that does **not** have the same volume as the other two.

1 mark

2) The distance from Arkton to Bealeham is 48 km. 8 km ≈ 5 miles.

What is the approximate distance between Arkton and Bealeham in miles?

 miles

1 mark

3) Isaiah does a paper round every day for two weeks.

He earns £3.15 for each paper round.
How much does he earn in total?

£

2 marks

4) The diagram shows Dawn's plan for her new garden.

She wants to build a fence around her garden.
How many metres of fencing will she need?

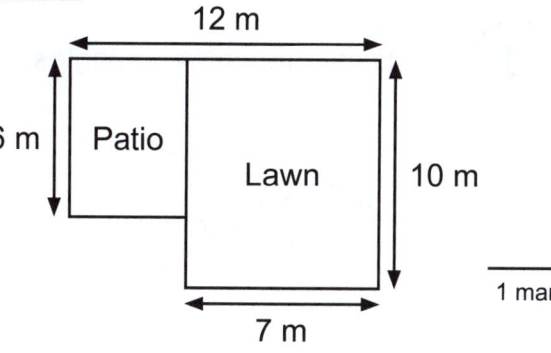

m

1 mark

Lawn turf costs £4 per 1 m².
How much will it cost Dawn to buy turf for her lawn?

£

2 marks

Check how well you've done with Measurement by adding up your marks from this Mixed Practice page. Write your score in the box on the right, then fill in the scoresheet at the end of the book.

/ 7

Section Six — Geometry

Angle Rules

1 Look at the angles on the right.

Give the letter of the reflex angle.

1 mark

Pick the best estimate for the size of each angle from the list below.

    34°   78°   110°   192°   245°

  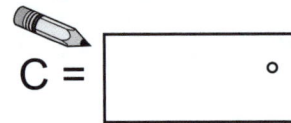

1 mark

2 Ansu says: "The sum of two acute angles is always greater than a right angle."

Explain why she is **not** correct.

1 mark

3 Calculate the missing angles. The diagrams are not drawn accurately.

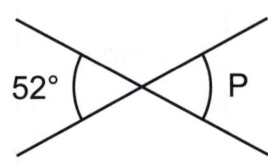 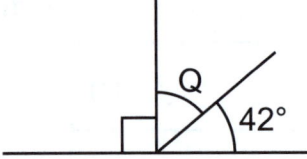 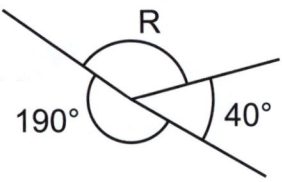

3 marks

"I can use rules to find missing angles."

2D Shapes

1) Circle **all** of the parallelograms below.

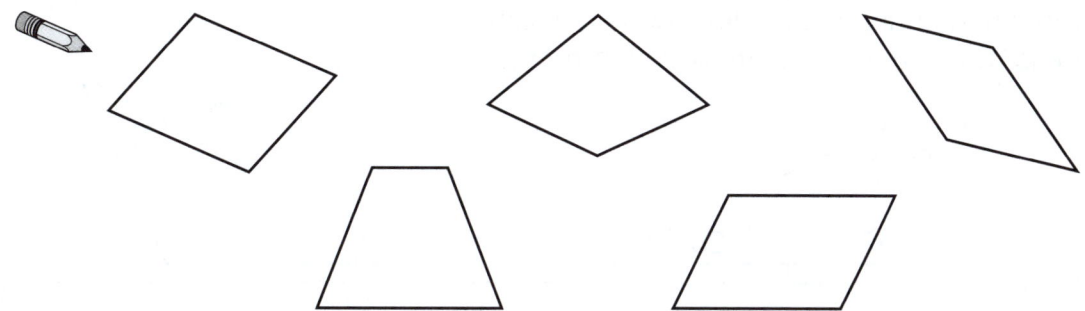

1 mark

2) Damien sketches the isosceles triangle below. It is not to scale.

Redraw the full size triangle **accurately**, using a protractor and a ruler. One side has been drawn for you.

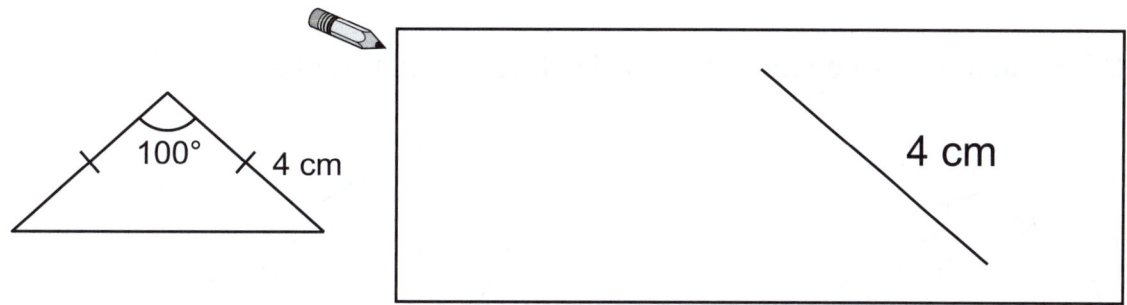

2 marks

3) Nia draws the circle below.

Write the names of the parts labelled A and B.

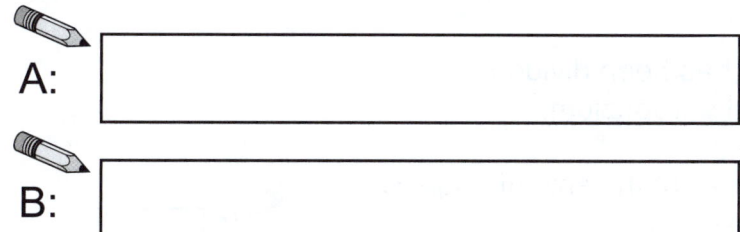

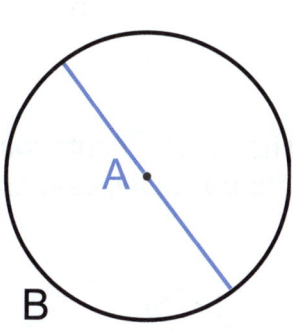

A:

B:

1 mark

Nia draws another circle with a radius of 4.5 cm. What is the diameter of this circle?

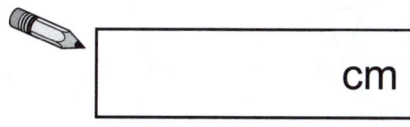 cm

1 mark

"I can draw 2D shapes accurately. I know the properties of different shapes, including circles."

Angles in Shapes

1 One of the triangles below has been labelled with the wrong angles.

Without measuring the angles, explain which triangle must have been labelled incorrectly.

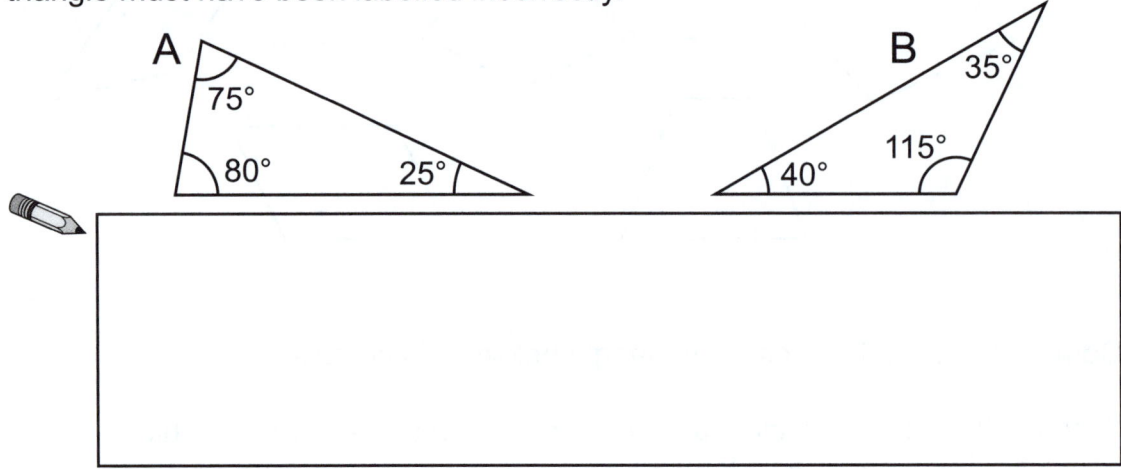

1 mark

2 Calculate the missing angles M and N in these quadrilaterals.

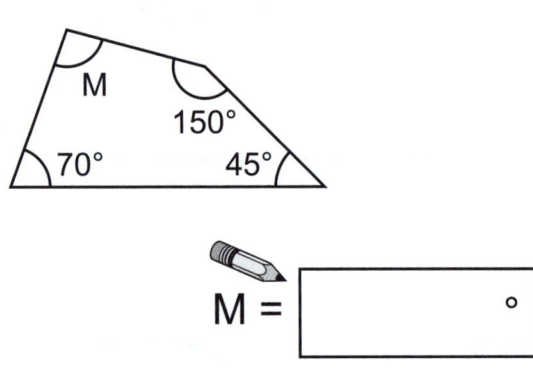
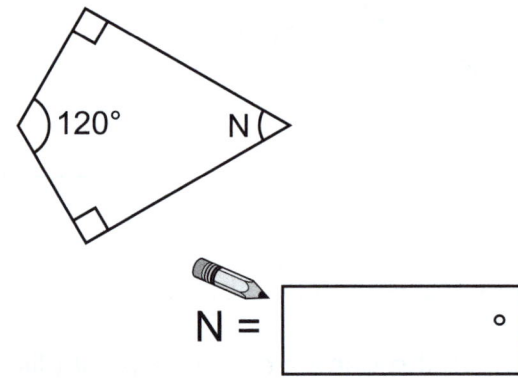

M = ☐ °

N = ☐ °

2 marks

3 The regular pentagon below has been divided into an isosceles triangle and a trapezium.

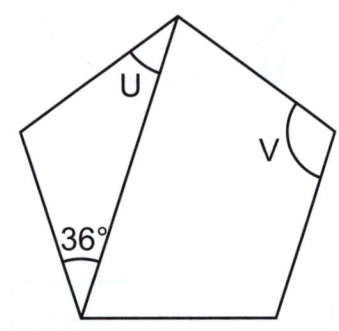

Work out the size of angle U.

U = ☐ °

1 mark

Work out the size of angle V.

V = ☐ °

2 marks

"I can use what I know about shapes to find missing angles."

Section Six — Geometry

3D Shapes

1 Look at the 3D shapes below.

Write down the name of each shape.

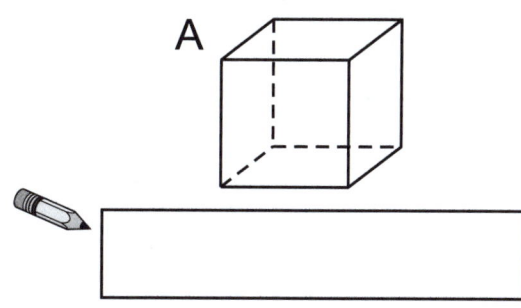

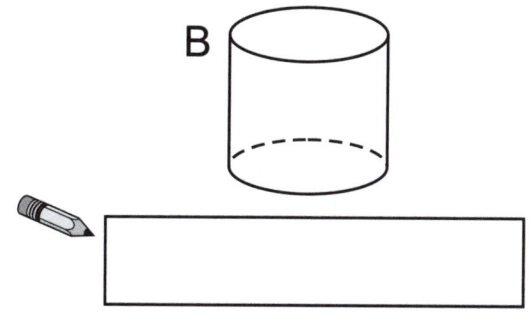

1 mark

How many more vertices than faces does shape A have?

1 mark

2 Draw a net for a 2 cm × 2 cm × 2 cm cube on the grid below.

1 mark

3 Circle the net below that does **not** fold up to make a triangular prism.

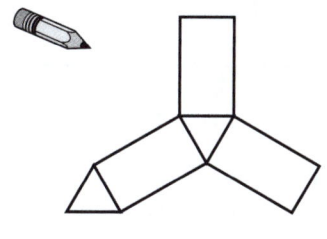 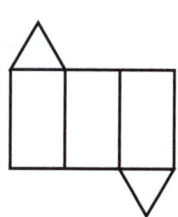 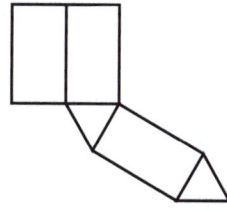 

1 mark

"I can recognise and describe 3D shapes.
I can draw nets of 3D shapes."

Coordinates

1) Write down the coordinates of the points plotted on the grid below.

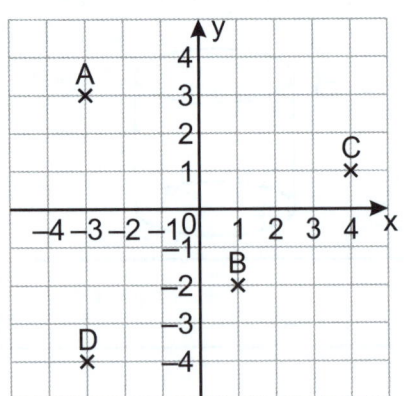

Point A (,)

Point B (,)

Point C (,)

Point D (,)

1 mark

2) A single point, P, is plotted on the grid below.

Plot the points Q(–3, 3), R(2, 5) and S(4, 3) on the grid.

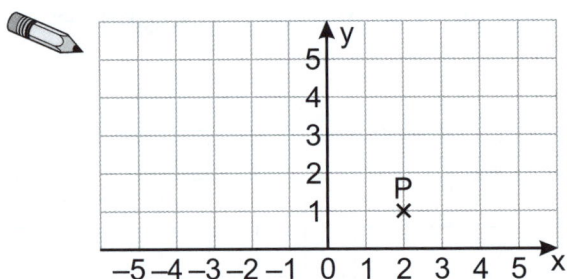

1 mark

What type of quadrilateral is the shape PQRS?

1 mark

3) F is the corner of a square and G is the midpoint of one of its sides.

Find the coordinates of point H.

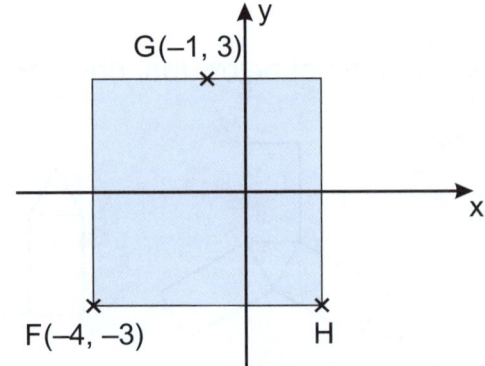

H = (,)

2 marks

"I can use coordinates in four quadrants."

Section Six — Geometry

© CGP — Not to be photocopied

Reflection and Translation

1 Reflect shape A in the vertical axis. Label the reflected shape B.

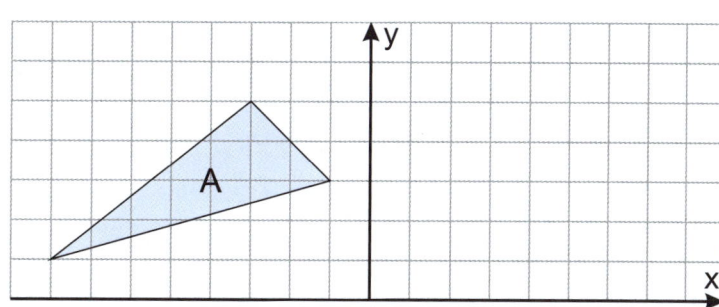

1 mark

2 Shape C is translated four units left and six units up to give shape D.

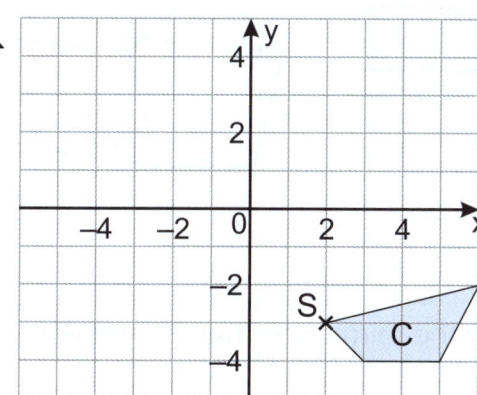

Draw shape D on the grid.

What are the new coordinates of the point S?

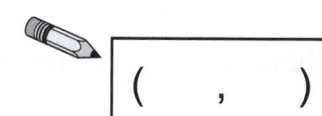

(,)

2 marks

3 Look at the diagram below. Shape F is a translation of shape E.

Fill in the boxes to describe the transformation.

Shape E has been translated:

☐ squares to the left and

☐ squares down to give shape F.

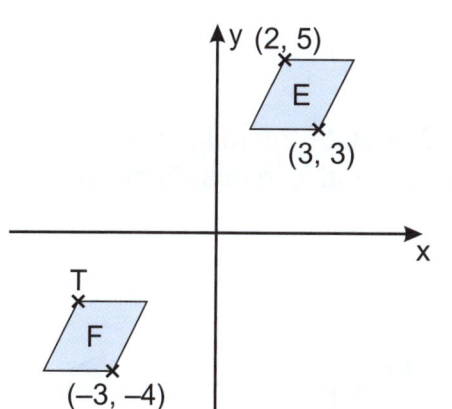

1 mark

What are the coordinates of the point T on shape F?

(,)

1 mark

"I can translate a shape using coordinates.
I can reflect a shape in the axes of a grid."

Mixed Practice

That's the end of Geometry — test how much you've learnt with these questions.

1 Draw a right-angled triangle that has exactly one 4 cm side on the grid below.

1 mark

2 Complete the table for the 3D shape on the right.

Number of...		
Faces	Edges	Vertices

1 mark

3 Shape Q is a reflection of shape P. Draw the mirror line that P is reflected in.

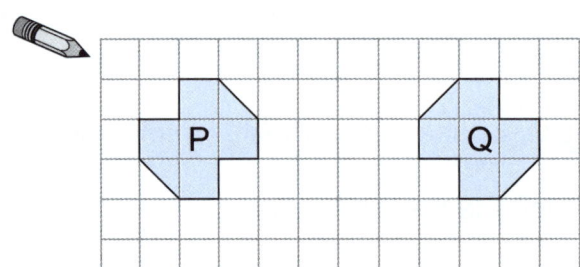

1 mark

4 Calculate the missing angles X, Y and Z in this diagram.

X = ___°   Y = ___°   Z = ___°

3 marks

Check how well you've done with Geometry by adding up your marks from this Mixed Practice page. Write your score in the box on the right, then fill in the scoresheet at the end of the book.

/ 6

Section Six — Geometry

Section Seven — Statistics

Tables and Pictograms

1 Henry and Jenny record the number of fish they catch each year. The table shows the number of fish they caught over four years.

	2016	2017	2018	2019
Henry	16	38	32	34
Jenny	18	22	15	13

In which year did Henry catch exactly twice as many fish as the number he caught in 2016?

1 mark

How many **more** fish did Henry and Jenny catch altogether in 2019 than in 2016?

1 mark

2 Geeta makes a pictogram to show the number of treats she gave to her dogs in one week.

Scruff	🦴 🦴 🦴 🦴
Pip	🦴 ⌒
Fuzzy	🦴 🦴 ⌒

Key: 🦴 = 4 treats

How many more treats did Geeta give to Scruff than to Fuzzy?

1 mark

3 Max needs to be in Sulverton by 3:20 pm. Look at this bus timetable.

Rabrow	13:33	14:19	15:05	15:51
Taldon	13:44	14:30	15:16	16:02
Sulverton	13:52	14:38	15:24	16:10

It takes Max 20 minutes to walk from his house to the bus stop at Rabrow. What is the latest time he can set off from his house?

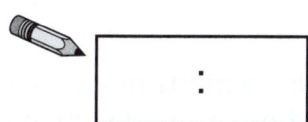

1 mark

"I can read and use information in pictograms, tables and timetables."

Bar Charts and Line Graphs

1 Mrs Steel asks each pupil in her class what their favourite fruit is. She uses the bar chart below to show her results.

How many more pupils chose banana than chose kiwi?

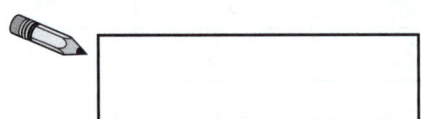

How many pupils did she ask in total?

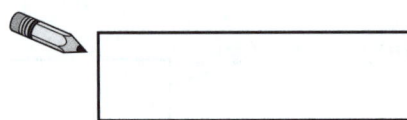

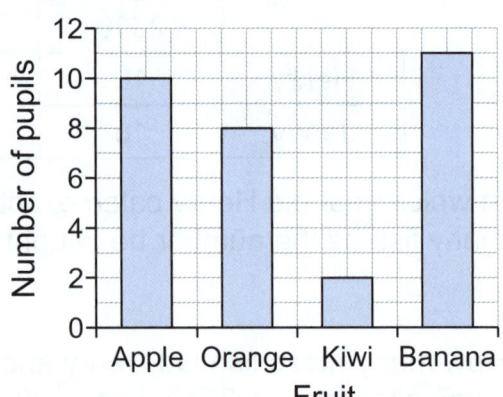

1 mark

1 mark

2 Derren measures the height of a sunflower every two weeks from the day he planted it. His results are shown on the line graph below.

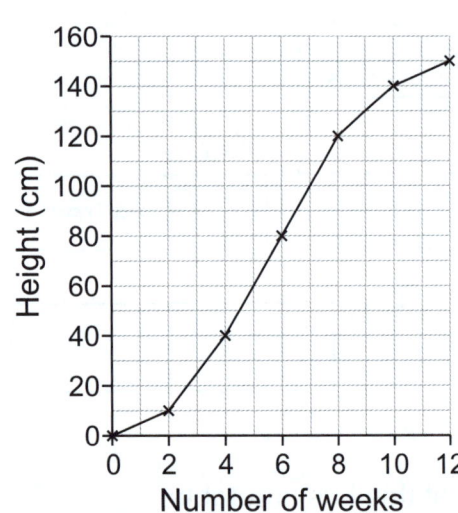

How much did the sunflower grow between the end of week 2 and the end of week 8?

 cm

1 mark

Estimate the sunflower's height 9 weeks after it was planted.

 cm

1 mark

3 The chart below shows the number of customers at a cafe over five days.

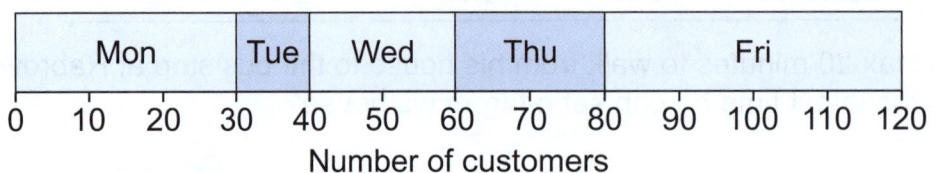

How many more customers were there on Friday than on Tuesday?

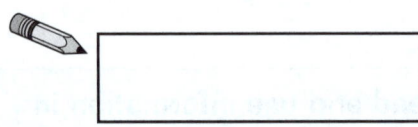

2 marks

Bar Charts and Line Graphs

4) Cara and Rav went birdwatching at a nature reserve. They recorded the number of birds they each saw at three locations on the bar chart below.

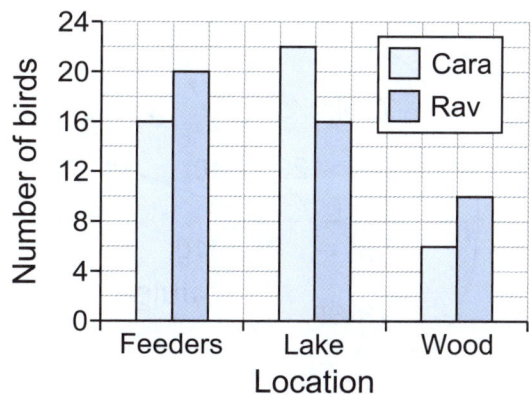

At which location did Cara see more birds than Rav?

1 mark

How many birds did Rav see in total?

1 mark

5) This graph shows the average monthly temperature in Noldon over a year.

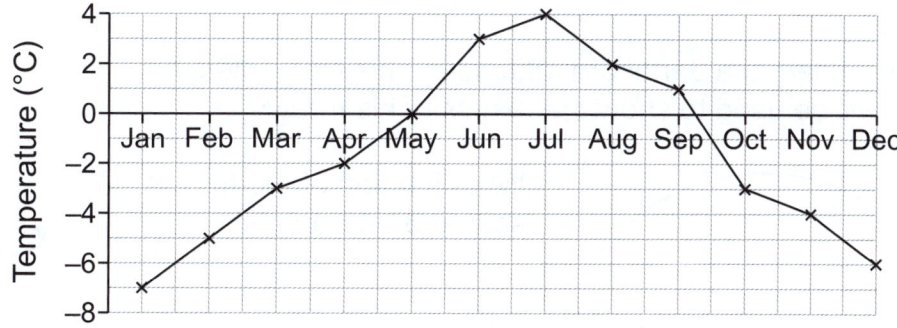

What is the difference in temperature between the warmest month and the coldest month?

°C

1 mark

"I can read line graphs. I can solve problems using data from line graphs and bar charts."

Pie Charts

1 Sasha asks the 36 guests at her party what they would like to drink. She makes a pie chart to show her results.

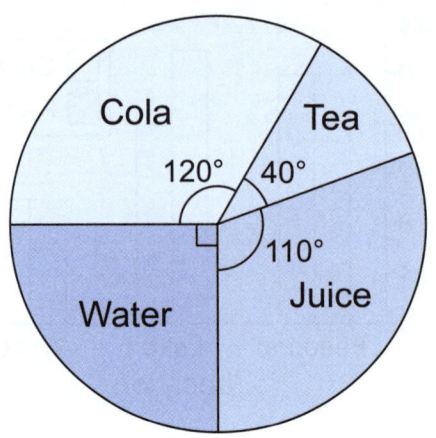

Which drink was the most popular?

☐

1 mark

Put a tick next to all the statements below that are **true**.

☐ Exactly four times as many guests wanted cola as wanted tea.

☐ One third of the guests wanted juice.

☐ 9 guests wanted water.

1 mark

2 Jing threw a dart at a dartboard 48 times. This incomplete pie chart will be used to show the results of his throws.

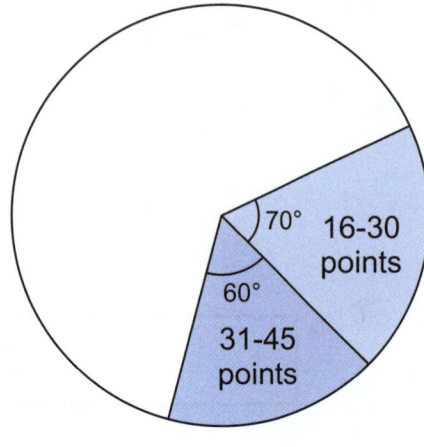

What fraction of the throws scored 31-45 points?

☐

1 mark

Jing scored 1-15 points on 24 of his throws. What size should the angle be for this sector?

☐ °

1 mark

"I can draw and read pie charts."

The Mean

1 Find the mean of the set of numbers below.

3, 6, 7, 9, 10

2 marks

2 The table shows how much money six pupils raised in a sponsored silence.

Name	Tim	Ayo	Sean	Emma	Keanu	Trisha
Amount (£)	7	12	16	9	5	11

What was the mean amount of money raised by the pupils?

£

2 marks

3 Kelly ran 7 km each day for three days and then ran 12 km each day for two days.

What is the mean distance Kelly ran each day?

km

2 marks

4 Imran and Hallie each drove three laps around a race track. They recorded their lap times in the table below.

Imran	99 secs	88 secs	83 secs
Hallie	97 secs	90 secs	89 secs

Who had the faster mean lap time? Show your working.

2 marks

"I know what the mean is.
I can calculate and use the mean."

Mixed Practice

That's the end of Statistics — test how much you've learnt with these questions.

1 This graph shows Jamie's distance from home whilst he was out on a walk.

How much further from home was Jamie at 10:00 than at 08:30?

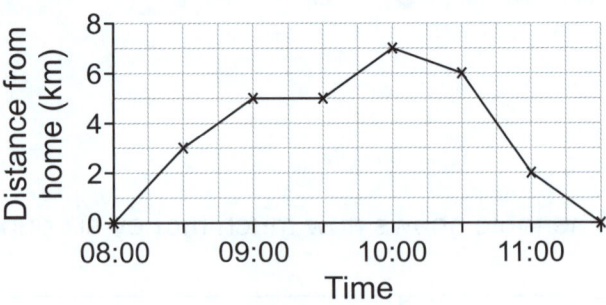

 km

1 mark

2 Fema draws a pictogram to show the number of sunny days in March.

There were 18 sunny days in March. Complete the key.

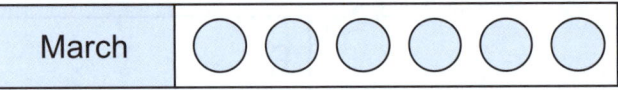

Key:
○ = 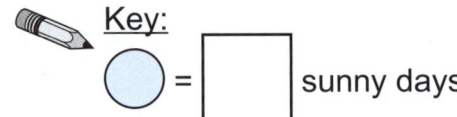 sunny days

1 mark

3 The pie chart shows the different types of act in a talent show.

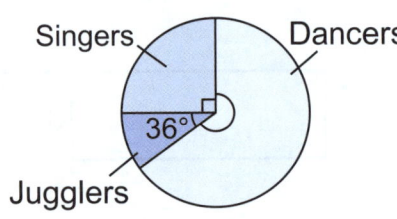

What percentage of the acts were jugglers?

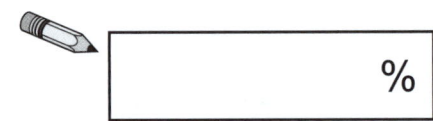 %

1 mark

4 The chart below shows the number of pupils in each after school club.

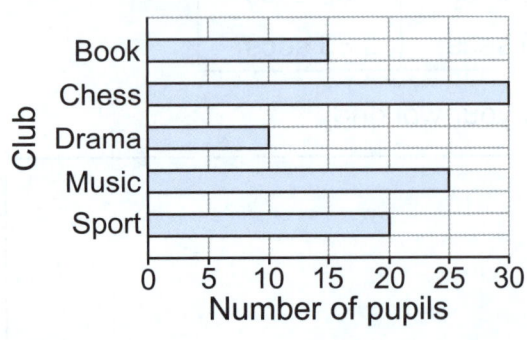

What is the mean number of pupils in a club?

2 marks

Check how well you've done with Statistics by adding up your marks from this Mixed Practice page. Write your score in the box on the right, then fill in the scoresheet at the end of the book.

/ 5

Practice Test

1 Look at the number 594.

Round 594 to the nearest hundred.

[   ]

1 mark

Write in words the number that is two hundred less than 594.

[   ]

1 mark

2 Kenny leaves his house at quarter to 5 in the afternoon. He gets back to his house two hours later.

Write the time that he gets back in the 24-hour clock.

[:   ]

1 mark

3 A carton of juice costs 45p.

What is the cost of 5 cartons of juice in pounds?

£ [   ]

1 mark

4 Circle all of the numbers below that are greater than $1\frac{1}{2}$.

1.4   0.9   1.06   1.501   1.49   1.6

1 mark

5 The triangle below is reflected in the horizontal axis.

What are the coordinates of the point A after the reflection?

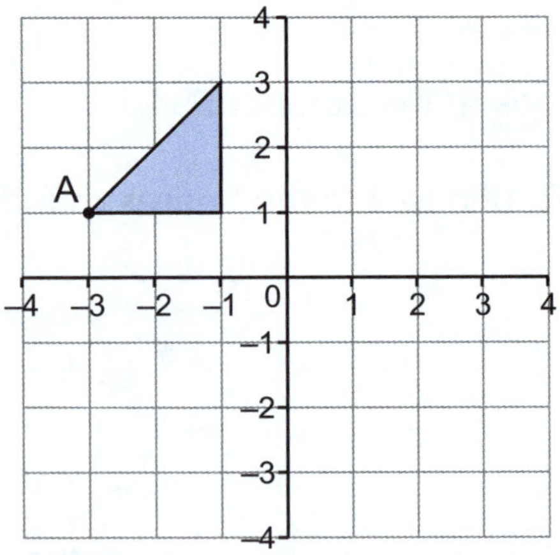

(,)

1 mark

6 Measure the obtuse angle in this triangle.

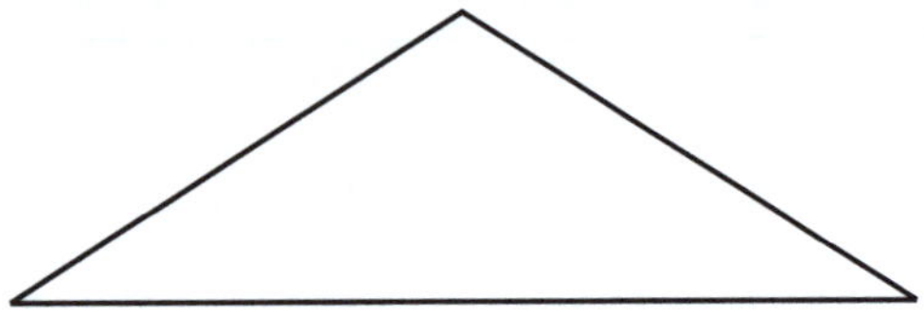

°

1 mark

7 Melanie makes this expression using some cards: | 7 | f | + | g |

What would be the value of the expression if $f = 5$ and $g = 15$?

1 mark

8 Keith has 10 bags, each containing three quarters of a kilogram of gravel.

How many **grams** of gravel does Keith have altogether?
Show your working.

g

2 marks

Practice Test

9 This net folds up to make a cube.

Shade the square that would be opposite square A when the net is folded up.

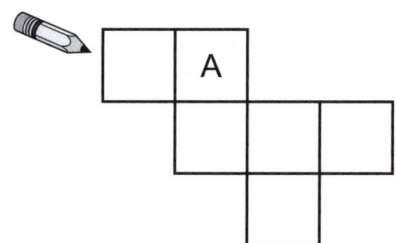

1 mark

10 Fill in the boxes in this puzzle with the correct numbers.

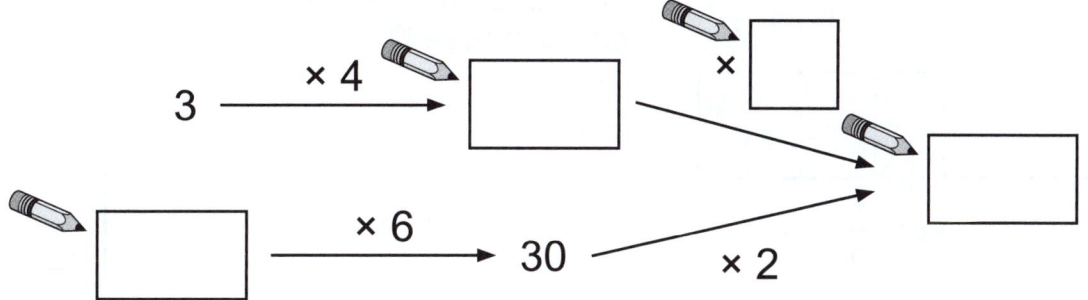

2 marks

11 The graph below shows how many people were living in a town over a number of years.

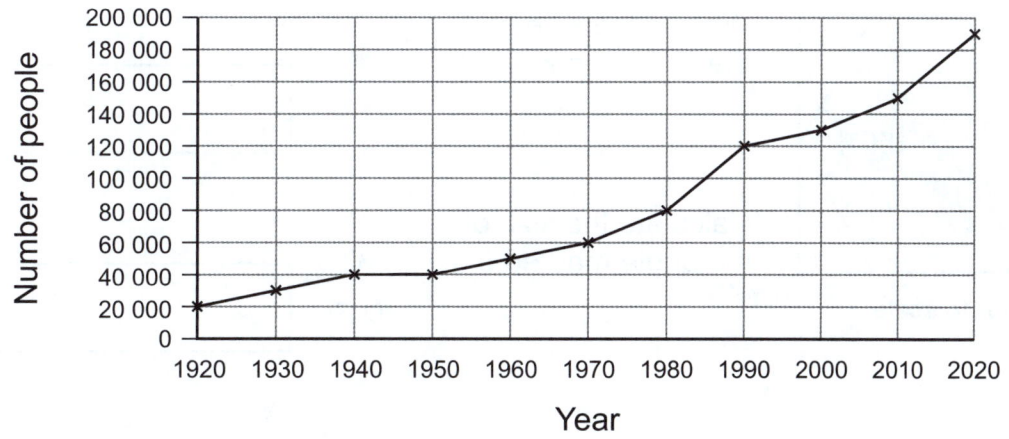

How many **more** people were living in the town in 1990 than in 1970?

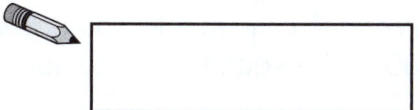

1 mark

How many people were living in the town in the year MCMXX?

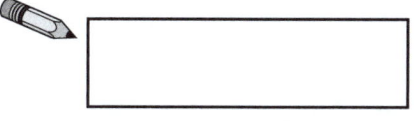

1 mark

12 Fill in each box with the correct **digit** to make the calculation correct.

10 + ☐ × ☐ = 45

2 marks

13 Sam, Len and Uma have raised some money for charity.
Len raised $\frac{1}{6}$ of the money and Uma raised $\frac{2}{5}$ of the money.

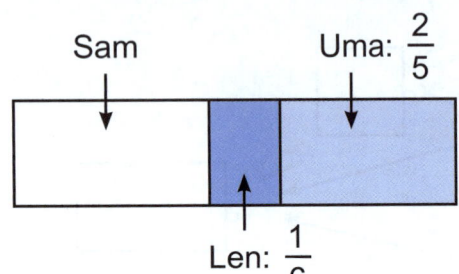

What fraction of the money has Sam raised?

1 mark

14 A regular hexagon has been drawn inside a rectangle.

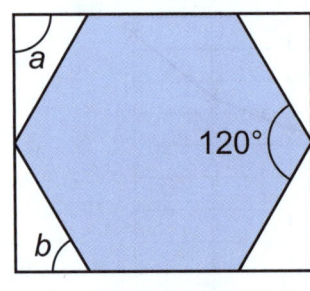

not to scale

What is the size of the angle marked *a*?

a = ☐ °

1 mark

Calculate the size of the angle marked *b*.

b = ☐ °

1 mark

15 A grid is divided into 150 equal squares.
30 of the squares are coloured red.

What **percentage** of the squares are coloured red?

☐ %

1 mark

16 Look at the table on the right.

What is the smallest square number that can replace:

P? Q?

	Odd number	Even number
Multiple of 5		Q
Not multiple of 5	P	

2 marks

17 The numbers in this sequence increase by the same amount each time.

Fill in the boxes with the correct numbers.

☐   −14   ☐   42   70

2 marks

18 This table shows the score that five people got in a quiz.

	Darren	Jane	Kris	Rish	Penny
Score	45	41	45	53	16

Work out the **mean** score.

2 marks

19 30 people were asked what type of home they live in. The pie chart shows the results.

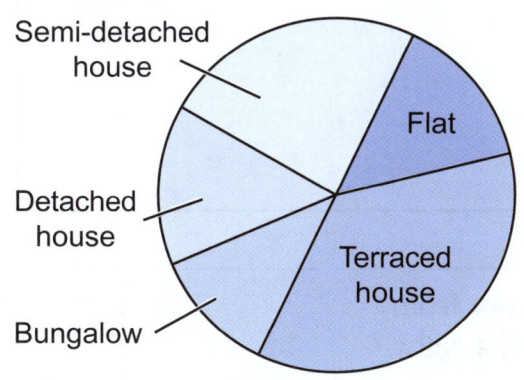

What is the total number of people that live in a flat or a terraced house?

1 mark

© CGP — Not to be photocopied

Practice Test

20 40% of this cuboid is filled with water.

What volume of the cuboid is filled with water?

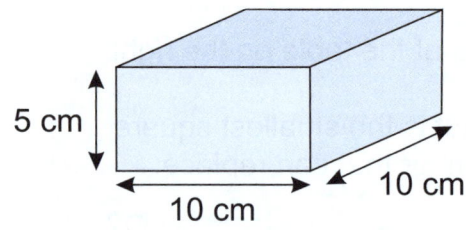

[ ] cm³

2 marks

21 The total capacity of 3 identical mugs is the same as the capacity of 2 identical bottles. Each bottle has a capacity of 0.45 litres.

What is the capacity of one mug in **millilitres**?
Show your working.

[ ] ml

2 marks

22 The rectangle and the triangle below have the same perimeter.

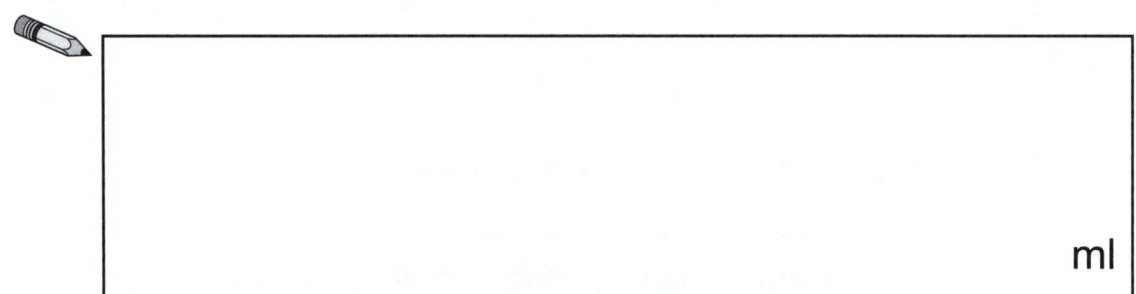

Work out the value of x.
Show your working.

$x =$ [ ]

3 marks

Check how well you've done by adding up your marks from this Practice Test. Write your score in the box on the right, then fill in the scoresheet at the end of the book.

/ 35

Answers

Section One — Number & Place Value

Page 2 — Place Value and Ordering Numbers

1) **8** *(1 mark)*, **500** *(1 mark)*
2) 247 in words is **two hundred and forty-seven** *(1 mark)*
3) **5296, 5353, 5359, 5378** *(1 mark)*
4) 594 + 6**0** = 654 *(1 mark)*
5) **200 000** *(1 mark)*

Page 3 — Negative Numbers

1) −11 + 8 = **−3** *(1 mark)*
   −3 + 6 = **3** *(1 mark)*
2) Count down from 5 m to water level at 0 m, and then count down 3 m below water level. So she dives down 5 + 3 = **8 m**. *(1 mark)*
3) −4 + 11 = **7 °C** *(1 mark)*
4) −9 + 5 = **−4** *(1 mark)*
5) −13 + 8 = −5, 2 − 7 = −5, so **−13 + 8 = 2 − 7** *(1 mark)*

Page 4 — Roman Numerals

1) X = 10, V = 5, I = 1, so XVI = 10 + 5 + 1 = **16** *(1 mark)*
   Wednesday = IX = 10 − 1 = 9
   Tuesday = VII = 5 + 1 + 1 = 7
   So he made 9 − 7 = **2** more cups of tea on Wednesday. *(1 mark)*
2) C = 100, I = 1, so ? = 50 = **L** *(1 mark)*
3) M = 1000, C = 100, L = 50, X = 10 and I = 1.
   MCCLXI = 1000 + 100 + 100 + 50 + 10 + 1 = **1261** *(1 mark)*
4) M = 1000, XC = 90, and I = 1. Malik will turn 90 years old in 1000 + 1000 + 90 + 2 = 2092. So 2092 − 90 = **2002** should be circled. *(1 mark)*

Page 5 — Decimals

1) **5** *(1 mark)*
2) **£1.89** should be circled. *(1 mark)*
3) 0.008 **<** 0.03 *(1 mark)*
   0.96 **>** 0.908 *(1 mark)*
   1.387 **<** 1.41 *(1 mark)*
4) 7 tenths > 5 tenths, so **Clark's** ladder is taller. *(1 mark)*
5) **0.332, 0.339, 0.34, 0.43**
   (2 marks for correct order. Otherwise 1 mark for the smallest and largest values in the correct place.)

Page 6 — Rounding

1) **927 410, 930 000** *(1 mark for both correct)*
2) **700, 4100** *(1 mark for both correct)*
3) **6 320 000** *(1 mark)*
4) **8 m** *(1 mark)*
5) **2.48** and **2.52** both round to 2.5 to one decimal place. *(1 mark for both correct)*

Page 7 — Mixed Practice

1) **238 855** *(1 mark)*
2) **2.3 m** *(1 mark)*
3) M = 1000, CM = 900, X = 10 and V = 5.
   So MCMXXV = 1000 + 900 + 10 + 10 + 5 = 1925
   So **2021** is bigger *(1 mark)*
4) Kerry won 2 games, which is 2 × 3 = 6 points, and lost 3 games, which is 5 × 3 = 15 points. So Kerry has a total of 6 − 15 = **−9** points.
   (2 marks for the correct answer. Otherwise 1 mark for a correct method.)

Section Two — Calculations

Pages 8-9 — Adding and Subtracting

1) 3 3 9
   +2 5 7
   ─────
    5 9 6 *(1 mark)*

2) ⁸9̷ ¹3̷ ¹5
   − 7 6 1
   ─────
    8 6 5 4 *(1 mark)*

3) 74 + 9 = 83 and 3 − 2 = 1, so 833 − 9**1** = 742 *(1 mark)*

4)   4 0 3 0
    +2 1 0 8
    ─────
     6 1 3 8 *(1 mark)*

     7 ⁷9̷ ⁸8̷ ¹5
    −6 1 3 8
    ─────
     1 8 4 7
   Paula has **1847 kg** left. *(1 mark)*
   You could also subtract 4030 or 2108 from 7985, then subtract the other one from the result.

5)   2 ⁷8̷.¹⁵6̷ ¹1̷
    −1 0. 7 8
    ─────
     1 7. 8 2 *(1 mark)*

6) **£25.48** *(1 mark)*
   E.g. £15.49 + £10 − 1p
   £14.52 *(1 mark)*
   E.g. £40 − £25 − 48p

7)   1 9.7 6
    +2 2.1 4
    ─────
     4 1.9 0 *(1 mark)*

     ⁵6̷ ⁹0̷.¹0
    −4 1.9
    ─────
     1 8.1
   He took **18.1 s** to swim the third length. *(1 mark)*
   You could also subtract 19.76 or 22.14 from 60, then subtract the other one from the result.

Pages 10-11 — Multiplying and Dividing

1) **0.513** should be circled. *(1 mark)*

2)   7 1 6
    ×   8
    ─────
    5 7 2 8   *(1 mark)*
      ₁ ₄

3) 90 ÷ 3 = 30, 30 × 4 = **120** *(1 mark for both correct)*
   160 ÷ 20 = **8**, 8 × 5 = 40 *(1 mark for both correct)*

4) She buys three tickets, so divide £18.99 by 3.
        6. 3 3
    3)1 ¹8. 9 9
   One ticket costs **£6.33**. *(1 mark)*

5)   9 3 r 3
    9)8 ⁸4 ³0
   She can make **93** bracelets. *(1 mark)*
   She will have **3** beads left over. *(1 mark)*

Answers

6) 1 box = 15 × 5 = 75 bananas
```
      7 5
   ×  2 7
   ─────
    5 2₃5
   1 5,0 0
   ─────
    2 0 2 5
      ¹
```
So he orders **2025** bananas.
(2 marks for the correct answer. Otherwise 1 mark for a correct method.)

7)
```
       1 9 0 r 6
   14 )2 6 6 6
     − 1 4
       ───
       1 2 6
     − 1 2 6
       ───
           0 6
```
Gino can fill **190** bottles.
(2 marks for the correct answer. Otherwise 1 mark for working using long division with no more than one error.)

Page 12 — Order of Operations

1) **3 × (7 − 2) + 8 = 23** *(1 mark)*

2) 6 + 3 × 5 − 9 = 6 + 15 − 9 = **12**
(1 mark for correct answer with correct working)

3) $12 - 2^2 \div 2$ ⟶ 4
   $(12 - 2^2) \div 2$ ⟶ 10
   $12 \div 2^2 - 2$ ⟶ 1
(2 marks for all lines drawn correctly. Otherwise 1 mark for at least one line drawn correctly.)

4) £1.20 × 3 = £3.60
   £3.60 + 70p = £4.30 *(1 mark)*
   £10 − £4.30 = £10 − £4 − 30p
   = **£5.70** *(1 mark)*

Page 13 — Checking and Estimating

1) **12.3** should be circled. *(1 mark)*

2) **47 × 16 = 752**
   or **16 × 47 = 752** *(1 mark)*

3) Estimate the answer, e.g. 1000 × 80 = 80 000, which is much smaller than 784 657. So it looks like Obi is **incorrect**.
(1 mark)

4) Use division, e.g.:
```
         3 3
   11 )3 ³6 ³3
```
(1 mark)

Page 14 — Multiples, Factors and Primes

1) **1**, **2**, **4**, **7** and **14** *(1 mark)*
   2, **7** and **11** *(1 mark)*

2) Factors of 12: 1, 2, 3, 4, 6, 12
   Factors of 30: 1, 2, 3, 5, 6, 10, 15, 30
   Common factors: **1**, **2**, **3**, **6**
(2 marks for all four correct common factors. Otherwise 1 mark for finding all of the correct factors of either number.)

3) The multiples of 7 between 40 and 50 are 42 and 49. Only 42 has a factor of 6, so the number must be **42**. *(1 mark)*

4) Multiples of 6: 6, 12, 18, 24, ...
   Multiples of 9: 9, 18, 27, ...
   So the common multiple that is less than 20 is **18**. *(1 mark)*

5) E.g. 165 = 5 × 33 = **5 × 3 × 11**
(2 marks for all three correct prime factors. Otherwise 1 mark for at least one correct prime factor.)

Page 15 — Mixed Practice

1) **2** and **11** *(1 mark)*

2) 8.1 × 10 = 81, 9.89 × 100 = 989
   So 8.1 × 9.89 = 80 109 ÷ 1000
   = **80.109** *(1 mark)*

3) £2.70 × 3 = £2 × 3 + 70p × 3
   = £6 + £2.10 = £8.10
   £8.10 + £4.59 = £12.69
   £12.69 − £10 = **£2.69**
(2 marks for the correct answer. Otherwise 1 mark for a correct method.)

4)
```
         4 2 5 r 10
   22 )9 3 6 0
     − 8 8
       ───
         5 6
       − 4 4
         ───
         1 2 0
       − 1 1 0
         ───
             1 0
```
There are **10** biscuits left over.
(2 marks for the correct answer. Otherwise 1 mark for working using an appropriate written method with no more than one error.)

Section Three — Fractions, Decimals & Percentages

Page 16 — Fractions

1) $\frac{2}{5} = \frac{6}{15} = \frac{8}{20}$
(1 mark for both correct)
   $\frac{7}{8} = \frac{14}{16} = \frac{49}{56}$
(1 mark for both correct)

2) $\frac{8}{14}$ and $\frac{12}{21}$ should be circled.
(1 mark)

3) E.g. [two-fifths rectangle] [one-quarter triangle]
(1 mark for both correct)

4) $\frac{23}{4}$, $\frac{18}{4}$, $\frac{13}{4}$, $\frac{41}{4}$, $\frac{11}{4}$
   $10\frac{1}{4}$, $2\frac{3}{4}$, $5\frac{3}{4}$, $4\frac{1}{2}$, $3\frac{1}{4}$
(2 marks for all lines drawn correctly. Otherwise 1 mark for at least two lines drawn correctly.)

Page 17 — Comparing Fractions

1) Make equivalent fractions with the same denominator, e.g.
$\frac{7}{12}$, $\frac{2}{3} = \frac{8}{12}$ and $\frac{3}{4} = \frac{9}{12}$.
So the order is $\frac{7}{12}$, $\frac{2}{3}$, $\frac{3}{4}$.
(1 mark)

2) Make equivalent fractions with the same denominator:
$\frac{4}{9} = \frac{8}{18}$, $\frac{6}{11} = \frac{42}{77}$ and $\frac{7}{8} = \frac{63}{72}$. So $\frac{7}{18}$, $\frac{6}{11}$ and $\frac{60}{72}$ should be circled.
(2 marks for all three correct. Otherwise 1 mark for two correct.)

3) $\frac{7}{8} = \frac{21}{24}$, so $\frac{7}{8} > \frac{19}{24}$ *(1 mark)*
   $\frac{14}{49} = \frac{2}{7}$, so $\frac{14}{49} < \frac{3}{7}$ *(1 mark)*

4) Make equivalent fractions with the same denominator:
$\frac{8}{24} = \frac{2}{6}$, $\frac{2}{3} = \frac{4}{6}$,
$\frac{5}{6} = \frac{25}{30}$ and $\frac{4}{5} = \frac{24}{30}$,
$\frac{5}{6} = \frac{50}{60}$ and $\frac{9}{10} = \frac{54}{60}$.
So $\frac{11}{6}$ and $\frac{9}{10}$ should be circled.
(1 mark for each correct fraction)

Answers

5) $\frac{7}{5} > 1$, so must be the largest. Make equivalent fractions with the same denominator, e.g. $\frac{18}{45} = \frac{2}{5}$, $\frac{24}{30} = \frac{4}{5}$. So $\frac{7}{5} > \frac{24}{30} > \frac{18}{45}$ *(1 mark)*

Page 18 — Adding and Subtracting Fractions

1) $\frac{1}{4} + \frac{6}{10} = \frac{5}{20} + \frac{12}{20} = \frac{17}{20}$ *(1 mark)*

2) $\frac{2}{3} - \frac{4}{7} = \frac{14}{21} - \frac{12}{21} = \frac{2}{21}$ *(1 mark)*

3) $\frac{1}{5} + \frac{3}{8} = \frac{8}{40} + \frac{15}{40} = \frac{23}{40}$
   $1 - \frac{23}{40} = \frac{40}{40} - \frac{23}{40} = \frac{17}{40}$
   (2 marks for the correct answer. Otherwise 1 mark for a correct method.)

4) $1\frac{3}{4} + 5\frac{1}{6} = 1 + 5 + \frac{9}{12} + \frac{2}{12}$
   $= 6\frac{11}{12}$ miles
   (2 marks for the correct answer. Otherwise 1 mark for a correct method.)

Page 19 — Multiplying and Dividing Fractions

1) $280 \div 7 = 40$, $40 \times 2 = 80$, so $\frac{2}{7}$ of 280 g = **80 g** *(1 mark)*

2) $\frac{5}{8} \div 3 = \frac{5}{8 \times 3} = \frac{5}{24}$ kg *(1 mark)*

3) $? \div 2 = \frac{2}{9}$, $? = \frac{2}{9} \times 2 = \frac{4}{9}$
   $\frac{2}{9} \times 5 = \frac{10}{9}$
   (1 mark for each fraction)
   $? \times 6 = \frac{4}{5}$,
   $? = \frac{4}{5} \div 6 = \frac{4}{5 \times 6}$
   $= \frac{4}{30}$ or $\frac{2}{15}$
   $\frac{4}{5} \times \frac{3}{7} = \frac{12}{35}$
   (1 mark for each fraction)

4) $25 \times 4 = 100$, $25 \times 20 = 500$, so $25 \times 24 = 500 + 100 = 600$
   $\frac{3}{4} \times 24$: $24 \div 4 = 6$, $6 \times 3 = 18$
   So $25\frac{3}{4} \times 24$
   $= 600 + 18 = \mathbf{618}$ **litres**
   (2 marks for the correct answer. Otherwise 1 mark for correct working.)

Page 20 — Fractions, Decimals and Percentages

1) $\frac{3}{100}$ should be circled. *(1 mark)*

2) $0.4 = 40\%$, so $15\% < 0.4$
   $\frac{17}{10} = 1.7$, so $\frac{17}{10} > 1.07$
   (1 mark for both correct)

3) $\frac{12}{25} = \frac{48}{100} = \mathbf{48\%}$ *(1 mark)*

4) E.g.
   Beth: $\frac{36}{50} = \frac{72}{100} = 72\%$
   Jordan: 75%
   (1 mark for converting values to fractions or percentages)
   So **Jordan** got the most questions correct. *(1 mark)*

5) $\frac{107}{200} = \frac{535}{1000} = \mathbf{0.535}$ *(1 mark)*

Page 21 — Mixed Practice

1) $2\frac{2}{3}$, $3\frac{1}{3}$, 4, $4\frac{2}{3}$, $5\frac{1}{3}$
   (2 marks for all three terms correct. Otherwise 1 mark for two terms correct.)

2) $\frac{4}{9} \div 5 = \frac{4}{9 \times 5} = \frac{4}{45}$ *(1 mark)*
   $\frac{4}{9} \div 8 = \frac{4}{9 \times 8} = \frac{4}{72}$ or $\frac{1}{18}$
   (1 mark)

3) E.g. 56 is a common multiple of 7 and 8.
   $\frac{3}{8} = \frac{3 \times 7}{8 \times 7} = \frac{21}{56}$ *(1 mark)*
   $\frac{6}{7} = \frac{6 \times 8}{7 \times 8} = \frac{48}{56}$ *(1 mark)*

4) E.g. Convert values to decimals:
   $\frac{60}{100} = 0.6$, $8\% = 0.08$,
   $\frac{1}{10} = 0.1$ and $\frac{4}{5} = \frac{8}{10} = 0.8$
   So from largest to smallest:
   $\frac{4}{5}$, 0.65, $\frac{60}{100}$, $\frac{1}{10}$, 8%
   (2 marks for correct order. Otherwise 1 mark for the smallest and largest values in the correct place.)

Section Four — Ratio, Proportion & Algebra

Pages 22-23 — Ratio, Proportion and Unequal Sharing

1) $8 \div 2 = 4$, $4 \times £3 = \mathbf{£12}$ *(1 mark)*

2) 10 miles = 5 × 2 miles
   So on the map, the towns are 5 × 3 cm = **15 cm** apart. *(1 mark)*

3) There are 6 times as many yellow flowers as there are blue flowers, so there are 3 × 6 = **18** yellow flowers. *(1 mark)*

4) 5 bowls weigh 200 × 5 = 1000 g.
   So 2 plates weigh 1000 g.
   So 1 plate weighs 1000 g ÷ 2 = **500 g** *(1 mark)*

5) 12 m in real life is 72 cm in the model, so 1 m in real life is 72 ÷ 12 = 6 cm. So 5 m in real life is 5 × 6 = **30 cm** in the model. *(1 mark)*

6) The length of 1 car is 48 cm ÷ 6 = 8 cm and 5 cars is 5 × 8 cm = 40 cm. So the row is 48 cm + 40 cm = **88 cm** long.
   (2 marks for the correct answer. Otherwise 1 mark for a correct method.)
   Alternatively, you could work out there were 6 + 5 = 11 cars in the row and 11 × 8 cm = 88 cm.

7) 1 watering can contains 72 litres ÷ 8 = 9 litres, so 3 watering cans contain 3 × 9 litres = **27 litres**. *(1 mark)*

8) X = 4 cm and Y = 12 cm, so the ratio of X to Y is **4 : 12** or **1 : 3**. *(1 mark)*

9) £2 + £3 = £5, £30 ÷ £5 = 6, so there are 6 lots of £5 in £30.
   Vic: 6 × £2 = **£12**
   Pearl: 6 × £3 = **£18**
   (1 mark for each correct answer)

Page 24 — Percentage Problems

1) 10% of 120 = 120 ÷ 10 = 12
   40% of 120 = 12 × 4
   = **48** *(1 mark)*

2) 50% of 320 = 320 ÷ 2 = 160
   5% of 320 = 160 ÷ 10 = 16
   45% of 320 = 160 − 16
   = **144** *(1 mark)*
   You could also have found 55% and subtracted that from 320.

3) There are 8 + 15 + 2 = 25 cars.
$\frac{8}{25} = \frac{32}{100}$ = **32%** are blue.
$\frac{15}{25} = \frac{60}{100}$ = **60%** are red.
$\frac{2}{25} = \frac{8}{100}$ = **8%** are silver.
(2 marks for all percentages correct. Otherwise 1 mark if at least one percentage is correct.)

4) Bob has 41 + 9 = 50 marbles.
$\frac{9}{50} = \frac{18}{100}$ = **18%** of Bob's marbles are green.
Katya has 16 + 4 = 20 marbles.
$\frac{4}{20} = \frac{20}{100}$ = **20%** of Katya's marbles are green.
(1 mark for either percentage correct)
So **Bob** has the lower percentage of green marbles. *(1 mark)*

Page 25 — Formulas and Combinations

1) **4 × n** should be circled. *(1 mark)*

2) **Apple and sandwich**
Crisps and soup
(1 mark for both combinations)

3) Price = 3 × £6 + £3.50
    = £18 + £3.50
    = **£21.50** *(1 mark)*
n = number of pizzas.
£45.50 = n × £6 + £3.50,
£42 = n × £6, n = £42 ÷ £6 = **7**
(2 marks for the correct answer. Otherwise 1 mark for a correct method.)

Page 26 — Finding Missing Numbers

1) Starting from 101, do the inverse calculations: 101 − 5 = 96,
96 ÷ 8 = **12** *(1 mark)*

2) ☐ = 45 − 27 = **18** *(1 mark)*
11 = 45 − △
△ = 45 − 11 = **34** *(1 mark)*

3) 64 ÷ X = Y, so X × Y = 64.
The two combinations are:
X = **2** and Y = **32** (or vice versa),
X = **4** and Y = **16** (or vice versa).
(1 mark)
The question says X and Y are different and greater than 1, so you can't have 8 × 8 or 1 × 64.

4) The only difference between the two patterns is ○,
so ○ = 186 − 141 = **45**. *(1 mark)*
Using Pattern B:
○ + 4 × △ = 141,
45 + 4 × △ = 141, 4 × △ = 96,
so △ = 96 ÷ 4 = **24** *(1 mark)*

Page 27 — Number Sequences

1) 16 − 9 = 7, so the rule is add 7:
9, 16, 23, **30**, **37** *(1 mark)*

2) 89 157 − 89 057 = 100,
so the rule is subtract 100.
89 357, **89 257**, 89 157,
89 057, **88 957** *(1 mark)*

3) **27**, 50, **73**, 96, **119**
(2 marks for all three terms correct. Otherwise 1 mark for two terms correct.)

4) 250 ÷ 50 = 5, so the rule is divide by 5: **1250**, 250, 50, **10**, **2**
(2 marks for all three terms correct. Otherwise 1 mark for two terms correct.)

5) 55 × 2 = 110, 110 − 5 = 105
105 × 2 = 210, 210 − 5 = 205
The sequence is 30, 55, **105**, **205**
(1 mark for each correct term)

Page 28 — Mixed Practice

1) 100 g = 40 g + 40 g + 20 g,
so the amounts in the scaled up recipe are two and a half times bigger (the scale factor is 2.5). There is 120 g flour in the original recipe, so there will be 120 × 2 + 120 × 0.5 = 240 + 60 = **300 g** in the scaled up recipe. *(1 mark)*
There is 250 g butter in the scaled up recipe. 2.5 × 100 = 250 g, so there must be **100 g** butter in the original recipe. *(1 mark)*

2) 81 − 64 = 17, so the rule is subtract 17: **98**, 81, 64, **47**, 30
(2 marks for all three terms correct. Otherwise 1 mark for two terms correct.)

3) 10% of 2100 = 2100 ÷ 10 = 210
1% of 2100 = 210 ÷ 10 = 21
3% of 2100 = 21 × 3 = 63
13% of 2100 = 210 + 63
               = **273** *(1 mark)*

4) n = weight of birdseed in kg.
£5.30 = 530p
530p = 50p × n + 30p
500p = 50p × n
n = 500p ÷ 50p = **10 kg**
(2 marks for the correct answer. Otherwise 1 mark for a correct method.)

Section Five — Measurement

Page 29 — Units and Conversion

1) **0.42 m** should be circled.
(1 mark)

2) 1.2 kg = 1.2 × 1000 = 1200 g
1200 ÷ 400 = **3** loaves *(1 mark)*

3) 0.98 m = 98 cm and
1.4 m = 140 cm, so the order is:
0.98 m, **119 cm**, **131 cm**, **1.4 m**
(1 mark)
1 foot ≈ 30 cm, so
5 feet ≈ 5 × 30 = 150 cm
              = **1.5 m** *(1 mark)*

4) 4.5 litres = 4500 ml
4500 − 750 = **3750 ml** *(1 mark)*

5) 5 miles ≈ 8 km, 15 = 5 × 3,
so 15 miles ≈ 8 km × 3
              = **24 km** *(1 mark)*

Page 30 — Time

1) 2 hours — 120 minutes
10 minutes — 600 seconds
2.5 days — 60 hours
144 hours — 6 days
(2 marks for all lines drawn correctly. Otherwise 1 mark for at least two lines drawn correctly.)

2) 22nd July + 9 days = 31st July
31st July + 12 days = 12th August
9 + 12 = 21 days = **3 weeks**
(1 mark)

3) 8:30 am + 3 hours 30 minutes
= 12:00 pm
12:00 pm + 3 hours 15 minutes
= 3:15 pm
3 hours 30 minutes
+ 3 hours 15 minutes
= 6 hours 45 minutes
= 6 × 60 + 45 = **405 minutes**
(2 marks for the correct answer. Otherwise 1 mark for a correct method.)

Answers

4) The time on the clock is 11:25.
11:25 + 2 hours = 13:25
13:25 + 47 minutes = **14:12**
(2 marks for the correct answer. Otherwise 1 mark for correct working.)

Page 31 — Money

1) 5037p = 5037 ÷ 100
    = **£50.37** *(1 mark)*

2) 90p + £1.22 = £2.12
£5 − £2.12 = **£2.88** *(1 mark)*

3) 80p × 8 = 640p = **£6.40** *(1 mark)*

4) £4.80 ÷ 4 = £1.20
£1.20 × 7 = **£8.40** *(1 mark)*

5) She spent £10 − £3.25 = £6.75.
So the original price of the jumper was £6.75 × 2 = **£13.50**
(2 marks for the correct answer. Otherwise 1 mark for correct working.)

Pages 32-33 — Perimeter and Area

1) Area = 12 cm × 12 cm
    = **144 cm²** *(1 mark)*

2) Count the squares in each shape.
Shape A = 5 squares = 5 cm²
Shape B = $5\frac{1}{2}$ squares = 5.5 cm²
So the answer is **5.5 cm²** *(1 mark)*

3) 21 cm ÷ 3 = 7 cm
7 cm × 6 = **42 cm** *(1 mark)*

4) Area of lounge = 4 m × 5 m
    = **20 m²** *(1 mark)*
Perimeter of kitchen
    = 4 + 3 + 4 + 3 = 14 m
1 m = 10 × 10 cm, so 10 tiles are needed for each metre. So she needs 14 × 10 = **140** tiles.
(2 marks for the correct answer. Otherwise 1 mark for the correct perimeter.)

5) To have an area of 36 cm², the side lengths must be a factor pair of 36. 3 cm and 12 cm give a perimeter of 30 cm.
E.g.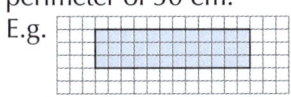
(2 marks for a correct shape. Otherwise 1 mark for a shape with either an area of 36 cm² or a perimeter of 30 cm.)

6) Area of parallelogram
= base × height
= 4 × 2.5 = 10 cm²
Area of arrow = 10 × 2 = **20 cm²**
(2 marks for the correct answer. Otherwise 1 mark for correct working.)

7) Area of triangle = $\frac{1}{2}$ × 15 × 2
    = 15 cm²
So the area of rectangle = 15 cm².
So the missing side length is 15 ÷ 3 = 5 cm.
Perimeter of rectangle
= 5 + 3 + 5 + 3 = **16 cm**
(2 marks for the correct answer. Otherwise 1 mark for correct working.)

Page 34 — Volume

1) Each cube has a volume of 1 cm³. Count the cubes in each shape:
Shape A = 11 cubes = 11 cm³
Shape B = 9 cubes = 9 cm³
11 cm³ − 9 cm³ = **2 cm³**
(1 mark)

2) Volume of cuboid
= 5 × 4 × 2 = **40 cm³** *(1 mark)*

3) Volume of carton
= 6 × 3 × 10 = 180 cm³
360 = 180 × 2, so the carton needs to be 2 × 10 cm
= 20 cm tall, which is
20 − 10 = **10 cm taller**.
(2 marks for the correct answer. Otherwise 1 mark for a correct method.)

Page 35 — Mixed Practice

1) 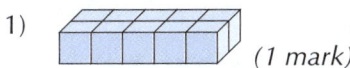 *(1 mark)*

2) 8 km ≈ 5 miles, 48 = 8 × 6,
so 48 km ≈ 5 miles × 6
    = **30 miles** *(1 mark)*

3)   3 1 5
  ×   1 4
    1 2 6₂0
    3 1 5 0
    4 4 1 0
      ¹
So £3.15 × 14 = 4410 ÷ 100
    = **£44.10**
(2 marks for the correct answer. Otherwise 1 mark for using an appropriate method.)

4) Work out the missing lengths:
12 − 7 = 5 and 10 − 6 = 4.
So she will need 6 + 12 + 10 + 7 + 4 + 5 = **44 m** *(1 mark)*
Area = 10 m × 7 m = 70 m²
Multiply by the cost per 1 m²:
70 × £4 = **£280**
(2 marks for the correct answer. Otherwise 1 mark for correct area of the lawn.)

Section Six — Geometry
Page 36 — Angle Rules

1) **B** *(1 mark)*
A = **78°**, B = **192°**, C = **110°**
(1 mark)

2) A right angle is 90° and an acute angle is less than 90°. Then, for example, **10° + 10° = 20° which is less than 90°**. *(1 mark)*

3) P = **52°**
Q = 180° − 90° − 42° = **48°**
R = 360° − 190° − 40° = **130°**
(1 mark for each correct angle)

Page 37 — 2D Shapes

1)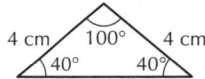
(1 mark for circling all three of the shapes above and no others)

2) The sides and angles should be the same as shown below:

     4 cm   100°   4 cm
        40°   40°

(2 marks for a correctly drawn triangle. Otherwise 1 mark for a triangle with two 40° angles OR two 4 cm sides.)

3) A: **Diameter**
B: **Circumference** *(1 mark)*
4.5 × 2 = **9 cm** *(1 mark)*

Page 38 — Angles in Shapes

1) Triangle A: 75° + 80° + 25°
= 180°, as expected.
Triangle B: 40° + 35° + 115°
= 190°, which is too big as angles in a triangle add up to 180°. **B is labelled incorrectly.**
(1 mark for identifying triangle B with a correct explanation)

Answers

2) M = 360° − 150° − 70° − 45°
       = 360° − 265° = **95°** *(1 mark)*
    N = 360° − 120° − 90° − 90°
       = 360° − 300° = **60°** *(1 mark)*

3) The triangle is isosceles,
    so **U = 36°**. *(1 mark)*
    The other angle in the triangle
    is 180° − 36° − 36° = 108°.
    All angles in a regular pentagon
    are the same, so **V = 108°**.
    *(2 marks for the correct answer.
    Otherwise 1 mark for attempting
    to calculate the other angle in
    the triangle.)*

Page 39 — 3D Shapes

1) A: **Cube**, B: **Cylinder** *(1 mark)*
    Shape A has 8 vertices and 6
    faces, so it has **2** more vertices
    than faces. *(1 mark)*

2) E.g.
    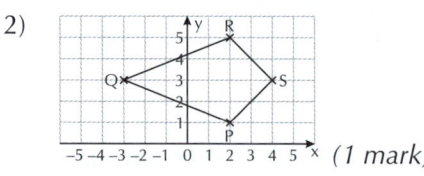
    (1 mark for a correct net)

3) 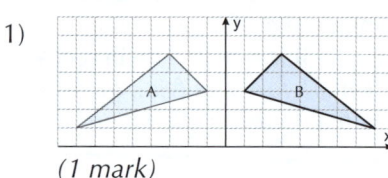 *(1 mark)*

Page 40 — Coordinates

1) A: **(−3, 3)**, B: **(1, −2)**,
    C: **(4, 1)**, D: **(−3, −4)** *(1 mark)*

2) 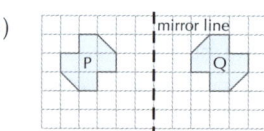 *(1 mark)*
    The shape is a **kite**. *(1 mark)*

3) The x-coordinate of G is halfway
    between the x-coordinates of
    F and H. −1 = −4 + 3, so the
    x-coordinate of H is
    −1 + 3 = 2. The y-coordinate
    of H is the same as the
    y-coordinate of F: −3. So the
    coordinates are **(2, −3)**. *(1 mark
    for each correct coordinate)*

Page 41 — Reflection and Translation

1)
    (1 mark)

2)
    The new coordinates of
    point S are **(−2, 3)**. *(1 mark)*

3) Shape E has been translated
    6 squares to the left and
    7 squares down to give shape F.
    (1 mark)
    T is the translation of (2, 5).
    2 − 6 = −4 and 5 − 7 = −2, so
    T = **(−4, −2)**. *(1 mark)*

Page 42 — Mixed Practice

1) E.g.
    *(1 mark for any right-angled
    triangle with one 4 cm side)*

2) | Faces | Edges | Vertices |
    |-------|-------|----------|
    | 7 | 15 | 10 |
    (1 mark)

3)
    (1 mark)

4) Angles on a straight line = 180°
    X = 180° − 115° = **65°** *(1 mark)*
    Angles in a triangle = 180°
    Y = 180° − 65° − 25°
      = 180° − 90° = **90°** *(1 mark)*
    Vertically opposite angles are
    equal. Z = **90°** *(1 mark)*

Section Seven — Statistics

Page 43 — Tables and Pictograms

1) 16 × 2 = 32, so the
    answer is **2018**. *(1 mark)*
    Add the values in the '2019'
    column: 34 + 13 = 47 fish
    Add the values in the '2016'
    column: 16 + 18 = 34 fish
    Subtract to find the difference:
    47 − 34 = **13** fish *(1 mark)*

2) Scruff: 4 × 🦴 = 4 × 4 = 16
    🦴 = ¼ of 4 = 1 treat
    Fuzzy: 2 × 🦴 + 🦴
    = 2 × 4 + 1 = 9
    So Scruff was given 16 − 9 = **7**
    more treats than Fuzzy. *(1 mark)*

3) 3:20 pm = 15:20
    The latest bus Max can get
    arrives at Sulverton at 14:38 and
    sets off from Rabrow at 14:19.
    It take 20 minutes for him to
    walk to Rabrow bus stop, so the
    latest time he can set off from his
    house is **13:59**. *(1 mark)*

Pages 44-45 — Bar Charts and Line Graphs

1) 11 chose banana and 2 chose
    kiwi, so 11 − 2 = **9** more pupils
    chose banana *(1 mark)*
    10 + 8 + 2 + 11
    = **31** pupils *(1 mark)*

2) At the end of week 2 it was
    10 cm and at the end of week 8
    it was 120 cm. So it grew
    120 − 10 = **110 cm**. *(1 mark)*
    9 weeks is halfway between
    8 and 10 weeks. Go up from
    9 weeks to the line, then across
    to the axis. The height was
    approximately **130 cm**. *(1 mark)*

3) Friday: 120 − 80 = 40 customers
    Tuesday: 40 − 30 = 10 customers
    So there were 40 − 10
    = **30** more customers on Friday.
    *(2 marks for the correct answer.
    Otherwise 1 mark for correct
    value for Tuesday or Friday.)*

4) **Lake** *(1 mark)*
    20 + 16 + 10 = **46** birds *(1 mark)*

5) The warmest month was July at
    4 °C. The coldest month was
    January at −7 °C.
    −7 + 7 = 0, 0 + 4 = 4, so the
    difference between −7 °C and
    4 °C is 7 + 4 = **11°C**. *(1 mark)*

Page 46 — Pie Charts

1) **Cola** *(1 mark)*
    Cola = 120°, which is 3 times
    as big as the 40° angle for tea,
    so the first statement is false.
    $\frac{1}{3}$ of 360° is 120° and the
    juice sector is 110°, so the
    second statement is false.
    The water sector is 90°,
    which is a quarter of the pie
    chart. This is 36 ÷ 4 = 9 people,
    so the third statement is **true**.
    (1 mark)

Answers

2) 60° out of 360° = $\frac{60}{360}$ or $\frac{1}{6}$
(1 mark)
$\frac{24}{48} = \frac{1}{2}$ so the 1-15 points sector should cover half of the pie chart.
360° ÷ 2 = **180°** (1 mark)

Page 47 — The Mean

1) 3 + 6 + 7 + 9 + 10 = 35
35 ÷ 5 = **7**
(2 marks for the correct answer. Otherwise 1 mark for suitable working.)

2) 7 + 12 + 16 + 9 + 5 + 11 = £60
£60 ÷ 6 = **£10**
(2 marks for the correct answer. Otherwise 1 mark for suitable working.)

3) 7 + 7 + 7 + 12 + 12 = 45 km
45 ÷ 5 = **9 km**
(2 marks for the correct answer. Otherwise 1 mark for suitable working.)

4) Imran: 99 + 88 + 83 = 270 secs
270 ÷ 3 = 90 secs
Hallie: 97 + 90 + 89 = 276 secs
276 ÷ 3 = 92 secs
So **Imran** had the faster mean lap time.
(2 marks for the correct answer. Otherwise 1 mark for calculating at least one correct mean.)

Page 48 — Mixed Practice

1) At 10:00, he was 7 km from home. At 08:30, he was 3 km from home. So he was 7 – 3 = **4 km** further from home at 10:00. (1 mark)

2) 6 × ◯ = 18
◯ = 18 ÷ 6
= **3** sunny days (1 mark)

3) 36° out of 360° = $\frac{36}{360} = \frac{1}{10}$
= **10%** (1 mark)

4) Add up the values of the bars:
15 + 30 + 10 + 25 + 20 = 100
Divide by the number of bars:
100 ÷ 5 = **20** pupils
(2 marks for the correct answer. Otherwise 1 mark for correctly calculating the total number of pupils.)

Pages 49-54 — Practice Test

1) **600** (1 mark)
Three hundred and ninety-four (1 mark)

2) Quarter to 5 = 16:45
16:45 + 2 hours = **18:45** (1 mark)

3) 45p × 5 = 225p = **£2.25** (1 mark)

4) $1\frac{1}{2}$ = 1.5, so **1.501** and **1.6** should be circled. (1 mark)

5)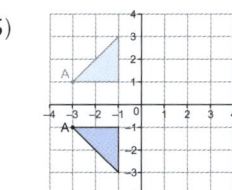
The reflection of A is at **(–3, –1)**.
(1 mark)

6) The obtuse angle is the one that is larger than a right angle:
115° (1 mark)
Allow answers from 114° to 116°.

7) 7 × 5 + 15 = **50** (1 mark)

8) Three quarters of a kilogram is 0.75 kg = 750 g. In 10 bags, there are 10 × 750 = **7500 g** of gravel.
(2 marks for the correct answer. Otherwise 1 mark for a correct method.)

9) (1 mark)

10) 3 —×4→ **12** —×5→ **60**
5 —×6→ 30 —×2↗
(2 marks for all four correct numbers. Otherwise 1 mark for at least two correct numbers.)

11) 1990: 120 000, 1970: 60 000
120 000 – 60 000
 = **60 000** (1 mark)
MCMXX = 1920
1920: **20 000** people (1 mark)

12) 10 + ? × ? = 45,
so ? × ? = 45 – 10 = 35
Factors of 35: 1, 5, 7, 35
The answers are single digits, so the missing digits are **5** and **7** (in either order).
(2 marks for the correct digits. Otherwise 1 mark for an incorrect factor pair of 35.)

13) $\frac{1}{6} + \frac{2}{5} = \frac{5}{30} + \frac{12}{30} = \frac{17}{30}$
$1 - \frac{17}{30} = \frac{\mathbf{13}}{\mathbf{30}}$ (1 mark)

14) a = **90°** (1 mark)
b = 180° – 120° = **60°** (1 mark)

15) $\frac{30}{150} = \frac{10}{50} = \frac{20}{100} =$ **20%** (1 mark)

16) Square numbers: 1, 4, 9, 16, 25, 36, 49, 64, 81, 100, ...
P is odd and isn't a multiple of 5. The smallest option is **1**. (1 mark)
Q is even and a multiple of 5. The smallest option is **100**.
(1 mark)

17) 70 – 42 = 28, so the numbers increase by 28 each time.
–14 + 28 = **14** (1 mark)
–14 – 28 = **–42** (1 mark)

18) Total score
= 45 + 41 + 45 + 53 + 16 = 200
Mean = 200 ÷ 5 = **40**
(2 marks for the correct answer. Otherwise 1 mark for the correct method.)

19) The Flat and Terraced house sectors take up half of the pie chart. 30 ÷ 2 = **15** (1 mark)

20) Volume = 10 × 10 × 5 = 500 cm³
10% of 500 = 500 ÷ 10 = 50
40% of 500 = 4 × 50 = **200 cm³**
(2 marks for the correct answer. Otherwise 1 mark for a correct method.)

21) Capacity of 2 bottles
 = 2 × 0.45 = 0.9 litres = 900 ml
So capacity of 3 mugs = 900 ml
Capacity of 1 mug
 = 900 ÷ 3 = **300 ml**
(2 marks for the correct answer in millilitres. Otherwise 1 mark for a correct method.)

22) The perimeter of the square is
6 + x + 6 + x = 12 + 2x
The perimeter of the triangle is
8 + 6 + x = 14 + x
These are equal to each other:
12 + 2x = 14 + x,
2x – x = 14 – 12,
so x = 14 – 12 = **2**
(3 marks for the correct answer. Otherwise 2 marks for setting the expressions for the two perimeters equal to each other. Otherwise 1 mark for one correct perimeter expression.)

Progress Chart

Put your Mixed Practice scores in here and see how you've done.

Section One — Number & Place Value	/ 5
Section Two — Calculations	/ 6
Section Three — Fractions, Decimals & Percentages	/ 8
Section Four — Ratio, Proportion & Algebra	/ 7
Section Five — Measurement	/ 7
Section Six — Geometry	/ 6
Section Seven — Statistics	/ 5
Total	/ 44

See if you're on target by checking your marks in the table below.

0-21	You're not quite there yet, but don't worry. Look at the progress chart above and work out which ones are your weakest topics. Really focus on those bits — you'll improve your Reasoning skills in no time.
22-34	Good job! You're doing well, but keep practising to make sure you're really ready for your test. If you spot certain Mixed Practice pages that you got a low mark in, go back and try that section again.
35-44	Well done — you've done brilliantly! Give yourself a huge pat on the back. Keep working hard and you'll be a Reasoning star.

Had a go at all the topics? Now try doing the Practice Test at the back of the book.

Practice Test	/ 35

0-17	You might need to do a bit more practice, but don't panic — try the questions again until you know everything inside-out.
18-27	Well done — you've done a good job! Make sure you practise your weaker topics and you'll be on track for a great score.
28-35	You're a whizz at everything Reasoning — congratulations!

Progress Chart | This page may be photocopied